Janet R. Price is direct[...] [...] Manhattan Borough President's Task Force on Education and Decentralization. She is the former managing attorney for Advocates for Children of New York, Inc. an organization that provides advocacy for New York City public school students. She has also served as a member of the Board of the National Coalition of Advocates for Students and was a 1986–87 Revson Fellow for the Future of the City of New York, at Columbia University.

Alan H. Levine, a constitutional lawyer, is a partner in the New York law firm of Steel Bellman and Levine. Formerly a staff attorney with the New York Civil Liberties Union and director of its Student Rights Project, Mr. Levine has taught constitutional law and has written, lectured and litigated in the area of student rights as well as in other areas of constitutional law. He is a member of the board of directors of the New York Civil Liberties Union and Chairperson of the Board of Directors of Advocates for Children.

Eve Cary, a former staff attorney at the New York Civil Liberties Union and senior supervising attorney at the Criminal Appeals Bureau of the Legal Aid Society in New York City, now teaches at Brooklyn Law School. She is the author of *The NYCLU Guide to Women's Rights in New York* and is co-author of a textbook on sex discrimination, *Woman and the Law*. She is a member of the Board of Directors of the New York Civil Liberties Union.

Also in this series

AN AMERICAN CIVIL LIBERTIES UNION HANDBOOK

THE RIGHTS OF STUDENTS

THE BASIC ACLU GUIDE TO A STUDENT'S RIGHTS

THIRD EDITION

Janet R. Price
Alan H. Levine
Eve Cary

General Editor of the Handbook Series:
Norman Dorsen, President, ACLU

SOUTHERN ILLINOIS UNIVERSITY PRESS
CARBONDALE AND EDWARDSVILLE

Copyright © 1988 by the American Civil Liberties Union
All rights reserved
Printed in the United States of America
Production supervised by Natalia Nadraga

95 94 93 92   5 4 3

Library of Congress Cataloging-in-Publication Data

Price, Janet R.
  The rights of students.

  (An American Civil Liberties Union handbook)
  Rev. ed. of: The rights of students / Alan Levine,
with Eve Cary and Diane Divoky.
  Bibliography; p.
  1. Students—Legal status, laws, etc.—United States.
I. Levine, Alan H. II. Cary, Eve. III. Levine,
Alan H. Rights of students. IV. Title. V. Series.
KF4150.P75 1988   344.73′0793   87-9890
ISBN 0-8093-1423-1   347.304793

Contents

Preface

This guide sets forth your rights under the present law and offers suggestions on how they can be protected. It is one of a continuing series of handbooks published in cooperation with the American Civil Liberties Union (ACLU).

Surrounding these publications is the hope that Americans, informed of their rights, will be encouraged to exercise them. Through their exercise, rights are given life. If they are rarely used, they may be forgotten and violations may become routine.

This guide offers no assurances that your rights will be respected. The laws may change, and in some of the subjects covered in these pages they change quite rapidly. An effort has been made to note those parts of the law where movement is taking place, but it is not always possible to predict accurately when the law *will* change.

Even if the laws remain the same, their interpretations by courts and administrative officials often vary. In a federal system such as ours, there is a built-in problem since state and federal law differ, not to speak of the confusion between states. In addition, there are wide variations in the ways in which particular courts and administrative officials will interpret the same law at any given moment.

If you encounter what you consider to be a specific abuse of your rights, you should seek legal assistance. There are a number of agencies that may help you, among them ACLU affiliate offices, but bear in mind that the ACLU is a limited-purpose organization. In many communities, there are federally funded legal service offices which provide assistance to persons who cannot afford the costs of legal representation. In general, the rights that the ACLU defends are freedom of inquiry and expression; due process of law; equal protection of the laws; and privacy. The authors in this series have discussed other rights (even though they sometimes fall outside the ACLU's usual concern) in order to provide as much guidance as possible.

These books have been planned as guides for the people directly affected: thus the question and answer format. (In some areas there are more detailed works available for experts.) These guides seek to raise the major issues and inform the nonspecialist of the basic law on the subject. The authors of these books are themselves specialists who understand the need for information at "street level."

If you encounter a specific legal problem in an area discussed in one of these handbooks, show the book to your attorney. Of course, he or she will not be able to rely exclusively on the handbook to provide you with adequate representation. But if your attorney hasn't had a great deal of experience in the specific area, the handbook can provide helpful suggestions on how to proceed.

Norman Dorsen, President
American Civil Liberties Union

Acknowledgments

Much of this book is drawn from the experience of the New York Civil Liberties Union's Student Rights Project, which for two years in the 1970s helped students in New York City public schools secure the rights discussed in this book, and of Advocates for Children of New York, Inc., an organization that works in a variety of ways to make the public schools more responsive to the needs of students and their parents.

The authors are grateful for the generous contributions of the Field Foundation and the New York Foundation, which made the NYCLU's Student Rights Project possible. We also wish to thank student advocacy groups across the country that are members of the National Coalition of Advocates for Students.

We particularly wish to acknowledge the contribution of Diane Divoky, who was coauthor of the first edition of this book; Ann Barcher, who did much of the legal research for the second edition; Susan Cockfield, who did much of the research for this edition; and Ira Glasser, executive director of the American Civil Liberties Union, for his early efforts in the field of student rights.

Finally, we thank the public school students themselves, for it is because of their courage and resourcefulness that the rights described in this book exist at all.

Introduction

The purpose of this book is to define the scope of school officials' power to regulate students' lives, and their reponsibilities to provide services and protections to students.

The following chapters outline the law in specific areas, but they all reflect a common theme: school officials can make and enforce only reasonable rules of behavior that are directly related to the students' education. They may not act arbitrarily. They do not have the power to control whom you date or hang out with in school or how you spend your free time. If you fall asleep in class because you were out all night at a party, you may be punished for sleeping, but not for partying.

School officials may not discriminate against you on the basis of race, ethnic background, sex, handicap, or ability to speak English. Although discrimination on the basis of sex, handicap, and lack of fluency in English are discussed here, one obvious omission in the book is a separate chapter on segregation by race. This is simply because the topic is so enormous and important that it requires a book of its own. (This book does, however, discuss racial discrimination in the chapters dealing with due process, corporal punishment, special education, and tracking.)

Racial segregation within the public schools has been a major political and legal concern of the nation since 1954 when, in the case of *Brown v. Board of Education*,[1] the United States Supreme Court ruled that separate schools for different races were by definition not equal, and segregated public schools were therefore in violation of the equal protection clause of the Fourteenth Amendment. Hundreds of cases involving different aspects of school segregation—*de facto* segregation, racial imbalance, freedom of choice, busing, token integration, housing patterns—have gone to the courts since that landmark decision, and most decisions have clarified or extended the rights of students to integrated schooling. The matter, unfortunately, is still not settled and will not be for many years to come.

It should go without saying that you have a right not to be discriminated against in school on the basis of race.

If you feel that you are meeting discrimination in your school because of your race (or for any other reason), you should take the matter to a community group that focuses on such problems or to a lawyer knowledgeable in segregation cases.

Most of the cases discussed in this book involve high school students, although a few college cases are mentioned. Most courts now agree that "the relevant principles and rules apply generally to both high schools and universities."[2] The same should be true of elementary and junior high schools, although few cases have actually considered the rights of students at those grade levels.

Most of the cases involve public schools and may not apply to private school students. A separate chapter discusses their rights.

Despite the developments in the law, you may still find that your principal continues to suspend students without hearings, keeps confidential records on students which parents are not permitted to see, and forbids student newspaper editors from printing satire on school policy because such criticism is "irresponsible journalism." Although those practices violate students' rights and would probably be declared illegal if challenged, rights do not have any effect merely because they exist in a lawbook. They are meaningful only if exercised.

When we say, for example, that a student has the right to go to school even though she is pregnant, we are aware that some schools still prevent pregnant girls from attending classes. That such a policy is illegal means nothing if it is not challenged.

Having said that, we should add a word of caution. Challenging practices that violate your rights can sometimes be costly. This may not make sense, since the law says that persons may not be punished for exercising their rights. But, as a practical matter, although a principal may not be able to prevent you from handing out leaflets on school property, he may be less than enthusiastic when it comes to recommending you for jobs or college.

That risk, of course, is not very different from the one that citizens always run when they exercise rights contrary to the interests or desires of those who have power to affect their lives. Southern blacks won the right to send their children to integrated schools in 1954; those who attempted to exercise that right sometimes found that they could not find work or get credit from local stores.

If you choose to exercise any of the rights described in this book and are penalized in any way, the local office of the ACLU might help. So might the support of your parents and your classmates.

In some areas, student advocacy groups or parent groups are prepared to assist. Legal services or legal aid offices sometimes assist in school cases, if some of the affected students are from low income families. Protection and advocacy organizations provide services to handicapped students. Civil rights groups and feminist organizations often come to the aid of minority students and girls.

As you read this book and think about your own school, it will be helpful to keep in mind the way the courts try to balance the rights of students against the power and responsibilities of school authorities. Some important decisions by the nation's ultimate legal authority, the United States Supreme Court, illustrate this point.

On the one hand, the Supreme Court has stated repeatedly that students do not shed their constitutional rights at the schoolhouse gate. On the other hand, the same court has repeatedly emphasized that public education depends on the discretion and judgment of local school administrators and that courts should not set aside their decisions lightly.

Some Supreme Court decisions are notable for emphasizing the constitutional rights of students. In *Tinker v. Des Moines Independent Community School District*, the Court made it clear that students enjoy First Amendment rights to free expression.[3] In *Goss v. Lopez*, the Court found students had a right to due process protections in the case of disciplinary suspensions.[4] Other decisions are notable for the rights they have denied. In *Ingraham v. Wright*, the Court ruled that students were not protected from corporal punishment in school, even though the Court had prohibited such punishment in prisons.[5] In *Bethel School District v. Fraser*, the Court ruled that a school could punish a student for language he used in a nominating speech for a school election. A majority of the justices did not want to second-guess the judgment of school officials that the language was disruptive.[6]

Some of the most interesting court decisions are the ones that try to strike a balance between individual students' rights and the school officials' authority and responsibility to maintain school discipline. In *New Jersey v. T.L.O.*, for instance, the Court decided that students were protected by the Fourth Amendment from unreasonable searches in school. But it worried that the strict limits placed on police searches would weaken school discipline. It therefore set more lenient rules for searches by school officials.[7] In *Wood v. Strickland*, the Court ruled that students can collect money damages from school officials who intentionally and maliciously deprive them of their constitutional rights or otherwise try to harm them. Students can also collect damages if the school officials did not act in good faith[8]—that is, if they knew, or reasonably should have known, that their actions would violate students' established legal rights. The Court criticized the lower court for second-guessing the school board's interpretation of its own rules and its weighing of the evidence against the suspended students. But the Court also said, "It is not the role of the federal courts to set aside decisions of school administrators which the court may view as lacking a basis in wisdom or compassion." In other words, students can collect if they can prove specific legal rights were *clearly* violated, but not just because the school authorities made an unwise or unfair decision.

It is important to remember that there are usually swifter and more effective avenues to achieve fair school policies than through the courts. You could try to be personally involved in setting school policies and could encourage your parents to participate. For instance, many school districts are required to have district-wide discipline policies and to involve parents and students in their creation. Student government and parents' associations offer a formal way to get involved, but you could also ask for a meeting about a problem or circulate a petition. Sometimes school officials need a polite, responsible reminder of the words of the Supreme Court:

That [Boards of Education] are educating the young for citizenship is reason for scrupulous protection of Constitutional freedoms of the individual, if we are not to strangle the free mind at its source and teach youth to discount important principles of our government as mere platitudes.[9]

NOTES

1. *Brown v. Board of Education of Topeka, Kansas*, 347 U.S. 483 (1954).
2. *Scoville v. Board of Education of Joliet Township*, 425 F. 2d 10 C 7th Cir. (1970).
3. *Tinker v. Des Moines Independent Community School District*, 393 U.S. 503 (1969).
4. *Goss v. Lopez*, 419 U.S. 565 (1975).
5. *Ingraham v. Wright*, 430 U.S. 651 (1977).
6. *Bethel School District No. 403 v. Fraser*, 106 S. Ct. 3159 (1986).
7. *New Jersey v. T.L.O.*, 105 S. Ct. 733 (1985).
8. *Wood v. Strickland*, 420 U.S. 308 (1975).
9. *West Virginia v. Barnette*, 319 U.S. 624 (1943).

THE RIGHTS OF STUDENTS

classes for them in Chinese, or to fashion some other means of giving them a good education, was discriminatory.[10] The Court noted that federal guidelines concerning discrimination in education provide:

> Where inability to speak and understand the English language excludes national origin–minority group children from effective participation in the education program offered by a school district, the district must take affirmative steps to rectify the language deficiency in order to open its instructional program to these students.
>
> Any ability grouping or tracking system employed by the school system to deal with the special language skill needs of national origin-minority group children must be designed to meet such language skill needs as soon as possible and must not operate as an educational dead end or permanent track.

Lawsuits in New York[11] and New Mexico[12] have also successfully challenged the lack of English language instruction or bilingual education for Spanish-speaking students and have required the school districts involved to provide such students with an effective educational program.

Federal legislation has also been passed to help guarantee that non-English-speaking students will receive adequate instruction.[13]

A true bilingual program provides instruction in English while teaching some subjects in the students' native language so that they can keep doing work at the appropriate grade level in math, history, and other subjects while becoming fluent in English.

Many proponents of bilingual education support a *maintenance* as opposed to *transitional* approach—that is, continuing to provide instruction in the native language as well as in English so that the student is completely literate in both languages and truly bilingual. This approach, called "developmental bilingual education" in the federal statute, is one of several program choices Congress has given to school districts.

The court in a leading case in Texas recognized that "schools are not free to ignore the need of limited English speaking children for language assistance to enable them to participate in the instructional program of a district."[14] The court created a now widely used three-part test for this assistance. First, the program must be based on a recognized educational theory. Second, the school system's practices, resources, and personnel must be adequate to put this theory into practice. Third, the school system must determine whether, over time, the program produces positive results.

Another court applying this test to bilingual programs in Denver found the school system had failed to take reasonable action to implement the bilingual education policy which it had adopted and ordered the schools to develop an appropriate remedial plan.[15] Parents and students in Bridgeport, Connecticut; Idaho; and Oakland, California, have successfully negotiated settlements with school districts that have agreed, among other things, to provide high school students with assistance in their native language in all major subjects at least three times a week, to increase parental involvement, to increase English instruction as students move through the program, and to plan for the education of students individually.[16]

At minimum, school districts must identify children who are not fluent in English; determine their language proficiency and relative academic achievement in English, where applicable, and in their native language; provide an educational program that enables them to make the transition into regular classes; provide trained personnel; and monitor the program to make sure it is both fully implemented and effective.

Can students who do not speak English be excluded from vocational programs?

No. The right of access to vocational and career programs has become an important right as these programs have become more popular with students in recent years. They are linked to actual jobs or college careers after graduation and are no longer automatically considered a lower track for non-college-bound students. Federal regulations prohibit discrimination on the basis of handicapping condition, limited English proficiency, gender, race, or national origin. They limit admission criteria to what is necessary to participate in the program.[17] A New Jersey case has made clear that schools may not discriminate against students who are not fluent in English in advertising vocational programs, accepting applications, and selecting students. English language tests may not be used to keep such students out of these programs.[18]

Can a public school charge fees for educational materials such as textbooks?

Although many public schools do charge students fees for educational materials, some courts have ruled that the practice is inconsistent with the guarantee of a free public education found in most state constitutions.

The Idaho Supreme Court, for example, in a case involving the withholding of transcripts from students who refused to pay a $25 annual fee, the proceeds of which went for textbooks and extracurricular activities, held that the fee constituted a charge for attending school in violation of the state constitutional guarantee of "a system of public, free common schools." The court further ruled that it is never permissible for a school to charge a textbook fee since textbooks are "necessary elements of any school's activity. . . ."

In answer to the school board's contention that withholding the transcripts did not prevent students from receiving an education, the court stated that a transcript is a "necessary incident" of a high school education and that not only school attendance but "the entire product to be received from it by the student must be 'free.'"[19]

The same reasoning would require a school to provide pencils and other equipment necessary for participation in regular classes. Similar decisions have been handed down by courts in North Dakota and West Virginia.[20] A court in Missouri ruled that schools could not charge registration and course fees in connection with courses for which academic credit was given.[21] Kentucky provides in its statutes that if sufficient public funds are not available to purchase and distribute texts in high school, reasonable rental fees can be charged to students, but no pupil can be denied the use of texts due to an inability to afford them and local school districts must establish a process to provide free texts to such students.[22]

Some state courts have ruled that fees are permissible. A Colorado court held that textbook rental fees could be charged,[23] a New Mexico court held that fees could be charged for non-required courses,[24] and an Illinois state court held that a provision of the state constitution requiring that students be provided with free textbooks did not prevent schools from charging fees to other students able to pay for other school supplies such as workbooks, maps, and laboratory supplies.[25] The Wisconsin Supreme Court and an Indiana court likewise held that a textbook rental fee did not violate the state's constitutional provision guaranteeing free tuition.[26] The Arizona Supreme Court went even further in holding that neither the state nor the federal constitution was violated by the refusal of the state to supply indigent students with free textbooks.[27] The U.S. Supreme Court refused to hear the case and the issue is still unsettled whether the federal constitution is violated by the refusal of a school to supply necessary books and equipment to students unable to pay for them. Given the Court's ruling in *Plyler v. Doe*, however, it would seem that if the inability to pay for books precluded the student from participating in school at all, the federal constitution would be violated.

Can schools charge fees for participation in extracurricular activities?

Courts vary widely on this issue. In Michigan, the state attorney general filed lawsuits against two school districts that charged fees for athletic participation. The court held that the fees were permissible since there was a confidential process through which students could apply for a waiver. Interscholastic athletics were deemed not to be a "necessary or integral fundamental part of education rising to the level which would require them to be provided at no cost" and no student appeared to have been arbitrarily prevented from participating.[28] The Michigan court distinguished between academic fees, which were prohibited, and extracurricular fees. But courts which permit fees for texts or courses would certainly permit fees for extracurricular activities.

In sharp contrast, the highest court in California found that extracurricular fees were prohibited by both the state constitution and state regulations.[29] The court said:

> [I]t can no longer be denied that extracurricular activities constitute an integral component of public education. . . . In addition to the particular skills taught, group activities encourage active participation in community affairs, promote the development of leadership qualities, and instill

a spirit of collective endeavor. These results are directly linked to the constitutional role of education in preserving democracy.[30]

The court concluded that any program that was important enough to be offered by public schools had to be offered free of charge:

The free school guarantee lifts budgetary decisions concerning public education out of the individual family setting and requires that such decisions be made by the community as a whole. Once the community has decided that a particular educational program is important enough to be offered by its public schools, a student's participation in that program cannot be made to depend upon his or her family's decision whether to pay a fee or buy a toaster. Nor may a student's participation be conditioned upon application for a special waiver. The stigma that results from recording some students as needy was recognized early in the struggle for free schools.[31]

NOTES

1. *R. R. v. Board of Education of Shore Regional H.S. District*, 263 A.2d 180 (Ch. Div. N.J. 1970).
2. *Hootch v. Alaska State-Operated School System*, 536 P.2d 793 (Ala. 1975).
3. N.J.S.A. §18A:38-1(b) (N.J. Education Department Regulations); New York City Chancellor's Regulation A-410 (1979).
4. *Rodriquez v. Ysleta Independent School Dist.*, 663 S.W.2d 547 (Tex. App. 8th Dist. 1983).
5. *Takeall v. Ambach*, No. 83 Civ. 9443 (S.D.N.Y. 3/26/85).
6. *Alford v. Somerset Cty. Welfare Board*, 158 N.J. Supr. 302 (App. Div. 1978).
7. *Plyler v. Doe*, 102 S. Ct. 2382 (1982).
8. 20 U.S.C. §2762(a)(1) as incorporated in 20 U.S.C. §3803(a).
9. *Zavala v. Contreras*, 581 F. Supp. 701 (S.D. Tex. 1984).
10. *Lau v. Nichols*, 414 U.S. 563 (1974).
11. *Aspira of New York, Inc. v. Board of Education of the City of New York*, 58 F.R.D. 62 (S.D.N.Y. 1973); *Serna v. Portales Municipal Schools*, F. Supp. 1279, *aff'd*, 499 F.2d 1147 (10th Cir. 1974).
12. Bilingual Education Act, 20 U.S.C. §§880b *et seq.* (1974); Equal

Educational Opportunity Act of 1974, 2c4(F), 20 U.S.C. §1703(F) (1974).

13. Bilingual Education Act, 20 U.S.C. §§880b *et seq.* (1974).
14. *Castaneda v. Pickard*, 648 F.2d 989 (5th Cir. 1981), 781 F.2d (5th Cir. 1986).
15. *Keyes v. School Dist. No. 1*, 576 F. Supp. 1503 (D. Colo. 1983).
16. *Zambrano et al. v. Oakland Unified School Dist. et al.*, (Alameda Cty. Superior Ct. 5/3/85); *Pagan v. Bridgeport Board of Education*, Civil Action No. B-82-120 (D. Conn. 2/21/84); *Idaho Migrant Council v. Board of Education*, 647 F.2d 69 (9th Cir. 1981).
17. U.S. Office of Civil Rights, "Vocational Education Programs: Guidelines for Eliminating Discrimination and Denial on the Basis of Race, Color, National Origin, Sex and Handicap," 45 C.F.R. Part 80, Appendix B.
18. *Berrios v. Camden City Vocational and Technical School*, Civil Action No. 80-3211 (D.N.J. 5/201/81).
19. *Paulson v. Minidoka County School Dist.*, 463 P.2d 935 (Idaho 1970).
20. *Cardiff v. Bismarck Public School Dist.*, 263 N.W.2d 105 (N.Dak. 1978).
21. *Vanderender v. Cassell*, 208 S.E.2d 436 (W.Va. 1974).
22. Ky. Rev. Stat. §157.110 (amended 1986).
23. *Marshall v. School Dist. Re #3 Morgan Cty.*, 553 P.2d 784 (Colo. 1976).
24. *Norton v. Board of Education of S.D. No. 16, Hobbs Municipal Schools*, 553 P.2d 1277 (N.Mex. 1976).
25. *Beck v. Board of Education of Harlem Con. School Dist. No. 122*, 325 N.E.2d 640 (App. Ct. Ill. 2d Dist., 2d Div. 1975).
26. *Board of Education v. Sinclair*, 222 N.W.2d 143 (Wis. 1974); *Chandler v. South Bend Community School Corp.*, 312 N.E.2d 915 (Ct. App. Ind. 3d Dist. 1974).
27. *Carpio v. Tuscon High School Dist. No. 1 of Pima City*, 524 P. 948 (Ariz. *en banc* 1974), *cert. denied*, 420 U.S. 982 (1975).
28. *Kelley v. East Jackson Public Schools and La Peer Community Schools*, 372 N.W.2d 638 (Ct. App. Mich. 1985).
29. *Hartzell v. Connell*, 679 P.2d 35 (Calif. 1984).
30. *Hartzell* at 43.
31. *Hartzell* at 50.

II

First Amendment Rights

Perhaps the most important of all rights guaranteed in our society is the right to express our opinions freely about problems and issues that affect our lives. That right is no less important for students than for adults. Most Americans between the ages of 6 and 18 spend nearly half their waking hours during most of the year in and around a school building. That is a large part of one's life, and the policies that govern the school have as much impact on students' lives as most policies formulated by the president and Congress have on the lives of adult citizens. It is as important, therefore, for students to be able to discuss school policies openly as for adults to be able to debate freely issues of national policy.

Of course, issues of national policy concern students, too, and they have a right to express their views on those questions as well. Women's rights, the environment, race relations, school busing, welfare, government corruption—these questions affect the lives of students directly, and they have the right to make their views known. If students have to wait until they graduate to do so, it may be too late for their opinions to have any impact. In the words of one federal court, "It is incredible to us that in 1972 the First Amendment was deemed inapplicable . . . to high school students living at the threshold of voting and dying for their country."[1]

Do students have the right to express their opinions on any subject while they are in school?

Yes. The U.S. Supreme Court, in a major decision, *Tinker v. Des Moines Independent School District*,[2] held that students do not lose their right to free expression under the First Amendment to the Constitution when they enter school. The Court explicitly rejected the position taken by some school officials that, once inside the gates of the school, students may be prevented from expressing themselves—whether on school policies or national events—unless the school wishes to permit such expression. The Court said that, on the contrary, students may be prevented from expressing their views only when they (the students) "materially and substantially" disrupt the work and discipline of the school.

The *Tinker* decision is important to read (it is set out in full in appendix B) because it is a clear-cut statement, applying to all schools in the country, of a student's right to constitutional guarantees in the school. The case involved students who were forbidden by school officials to wear black armbands in school to protest the war in Vietnam. The Supreme Court's decision does not merely protect armbands but is intended to apply generally to other means of expressing views. Other courts have applied the legal principles set forth in the *Tinker* decision to such forms of expression as newspapers, leaflets, buttons, and political clubs.

The *Tinker* decision is also significant because in it the Supreme Court recognized that the First Amendment right to free expression has an important place in our public schools. In other words, the First Amendment is not just to be grudgingly tolerated in school: it is fundamental to the American theory of education. As the Court pointed out, "personal intercommunication among the students"—on subjects that may not be officially approved—is as much a part of the educational process as formal classroom teaching.

At this point we must once again warn that exercising your First Amendment rights involves risks. School officials sometimes defy the law, and reasonable people can disagree in specific situations as to whether the expression of views is "substantially disruptive." You may be acting within your rights, but you also may have to go to court to prove it. For example, despite the *Tinker* ruling, a Texas school superintendent prohibited students from wearing armbands on one of the Vietnam moratorium days because he had heard that there were going to be disruptions at various schools. A court ultimately overruled the superintendent because there was no evidence to support his fears that the armbands themselves would cause the disruptions, but the students went through a hard fight.[3]

If you're in doubt about the legality of a planned action, you may want to consider whether there are less risky but still effective means of making your point. Ultimately, you may want to consult a lawyer.

Can students be prohibited from expressing their views if those who hold opposing views become angry and boisterous?

No. Once *Tinker* established the test of material and substantial disruption as a standard for First Amendment activity, some courts were faced with situations where, although the students who expressed their views were perfectly orderly, those who took exception to those views became threatening and disorderly. Quite reasonably, the courts have consistently held that the rights of those who peacefully express their views may not so easily be defeated. Thus, when school officials attempted to ban distribution of a student newspaper because of the hostility of other students, the court said that if the student distributed the newspaper in an "orderly, non-disruptive manner, then he should not suffer if other students, who are lacking in self-control, tend to over-react, thereby becoming a disruptive influence."[4] Perhaps where tensions at a school are very high, then regulation of "time, place, and manner" of expression of views might be permitted because of the fear of other students' reactions.[5] But "the administration should, of course, take all reasonable steps to control disturbances, however generated."[6]

In a Texas case[7] where the school superintendent barred the wearing of armbands because of rumors of planned disruptions, the court warned school officials against basing their fear of disruption merely on "intuition" and gave this advice to school officials who too hastily prohibited students from expressing their views: "We believe that the Supreme Court [in *Tinker*] has declared a constitutional right which school authorities must nurture and protect, not extinguish, unless they find the circumstances allow them no practical alternative."

In a case involving a somewhat similar issue, a federal court of appeals ruled that while a lower court's prohibition against the use of the name "Rebels" and of the confederate flag as the symbols of a recently desegregated school did not violate the First Amendment rights of the students in light of the serious problem of racial violence in the school, the prohibition should not be permanent and should last only as long as absolutely necessary to prevent disruption.[8]

Can students wear buttons and other symbols to express their views?

Usually yes, since wearing a button rarely disrupts any school activity.[9] However, one court refused to permit students to wear buttons because those handing out the buttons were being noisy and stopping other students in the hall.[10] In another case, students were not allowed to wear buttons because, in the past, students had worn racially inflammatory buttons that had caused tensions and disruptions at the school.[11]

Similarly, another court upheld a school principal's ban on the wearing of armbands bearing the words "strike," "rally," and "stop the killing" just after the United States' invasion of Cambodia and the killing of four students at Kent State University by National Guardsmen. The court found that the school body was divided on these issues and that a potentially disruptive situation existed which would justify a temporary restriction on certain types of armbands.[12]

These situations are unusual, however, and the school can almost never legally restrict the wearing of any button or other insignia. The mere fact that someone finds the message on your button offensive is not a valid reason to keep you from wearing it.

Can students use school facilities such as bulletin boards, loudspeakers, mimeograph machines, and meeting rooms to express their views?

If the use of these school facilities for expression of student views would not be likely to disrupt regular school activities, students should be able to use them. However, a school may legitimately refuse to allow students to use its mimeograph machine if, for example, it is used all day long in the preparation of course material. If the loudspeaker is used only for school business, such as the announcement of school activities, program changes, and special events, a court would probably hold that student groups may legally be prevented from using it for the expression of particular opinions. On the other hand, facilities such as bulletin boards should present no problem since space for the use of students can almost always be made available.

Of course, if any facility is made available to one group, the school may not then deny other groups the opportunity to use that facility. Thus, a court held that it was unconstitutional for school officials to refuse to distribute notices informing parents of probusing rallies when those officials had previously agreed to distribute notices about antibusing rallies.[13]

In another case, an antiwar organization had been denied

permission by the school board to provide students with information regarding legal alternatives to the draft and military service even though representatives of the armed services were permitted to provide students with information about military careers. In some schools, the military recruiters were permitted to distribute literature, post notices, place ads in school papers, conduct workshops, provide counseling, and administer tests. The court held that the school board's policy was unconstitutional because it favored one point of view over another. The court ordered that the antiwar organization be given the same access to students and school facilities as was given to the military recruiters.[14]

In 1984, Congress passed the Equal Access Act, which makes it unlawful for any public secondary school to deny to any student group wishing to conduct a meeting equal access to school facilities on the basis of the content of the speech at that meeting.[15] Although there have been few cases interpreting that act, it may be that the act will strengthen the right of students to use school facilities for meetings.[16]

Can school officials keep students from forming an after-school club having an unpopular point of view?

No, unless the officials, applying the *Tinker* formula, can show that the club will "materially and substantially" disrupt school activities.

The right to form groups and associations has for years been recognized by the courts to be an important aspect of one's right to express one's views.[17] For example, forming a club in school might allow you to use various school facilities, such as bulletin boards, loudspeakers, and meeting rooms, or allow you to present a school assembly. One school that had a policy barring clubs representing a "partisan" point of view wouldn't give recognition to a high school chapter of the Student Mobilization Committee. A court overruled the school administration, saying, as the Supreme Court did in *Tinker*, that the organization would make a substantial contribution to the educational process through the expression of its point of view.[18]

The Supreme Court ruled in a similar case that a college could not deny official recognition to a chapter of Students for a Democratic Society (SDS) unless it could be shown that the aims of the chapter were to disrupt the school.[19]

In a similar case involving high school students, a federal court ruled that "absent a threat to the orderly operation of the school, to deny recognition to a student group for the reason that it advocates 'controversial' ideas is patently unconstitutional."[20]

Another court ordered the administrators of a state college to register a gay students' organization and afford the group the same privileges that normally follow from registration.[21] Those privileges included listing the organization in the student directory, use of meeting space in university facilities, access to campus bulletin boards, and eligibility for college funding for organizational activities.

Can a school prevent a student organization from holding a social event?

In a case brought by a gay students' organization, a federal court of appeals held that a university's prohibition against the organization's holding social functions on campus denied gay students their First Amendment right of free association.[22] The university administrators argued that as long as they permitted the group to hold meetings, they could ban social events which they believed to be "not among the class of protected associational activities." The court disagreed, however, citing the "important role that social events can play in individuals' efforts to associate and further their common beliefs."

Can a school prevent students from inviting a speaker to their club meeting because he or she is too controversial?

No. If clubs are allowed to meet and to decide upon their own programs, then they cannot be denied the right to invite a particular outside speaker because of his or her views, unless the school can show that the speech is likely to create disorder at the school.[23] The fear of disorder, moreover, must be founded on "clear and convincing" evidence and not on speculation based on the speaker's known radical views.

Can students be penalized for picketing outside the school, or for walking out of class, or sitting in, if the demonstration is peaceful and orderly?

The First Amendment protects "peaceable assembly," a provision generally applied to peaceful and orderly demonstrations. When it comes to demonstrations on school property, most court decisions have been unfavorable, particularly when the demonstration takes place during school hours or inside a school building. Under the *Tinker* test, it is more likely that such demonstrations will be found to "materially and substantially disrupt" school activities.

One court, for example, upheld the suspension of a group of black students who walked out of a school pep rally when the song "Dixie" was played.[24] School officials had found the walkout disruptive. In another case, a federal court held that students could be suspended for staying out of school and conducting a rally to protest school policies that they claimed were racially discriminatory.[25] And still another court permitted a school to prohibit all demonstrations inside any school building.[26] Under *Tinker*, this decision seems clearly wrong because the court made no distinction between demonstrations which disrupt school activities and those which do not.

A Pennsylvania court analyzed the problem better. Even though it upheld suspensions for an in-school sit-in, the court stated that a sit-in was not illegal merely because it was indoors; or because other students gathered in the halls to watch; or because school administrators, who had chosen to keep watch on the demonstration, could not attend to their duties. The court said that in deciding under the *Tinker* test when a demonstration "materially" interferes with school activities, "the courts can only consider the conduct of the demonstrators and not the reaction of the audience."[27] The Pennsylvania court found, however, that this particular demonstration did materially interfere with school activities because the student demonstrators missed scheduled classes, and noise from the demonstration required some classes to be moved to different locations and disturbed others.

A demonstration outside the school building, such as a rally or picketing, has more chance of being found legal than one inside the building. The test, again, is material and substantial disruption of school activities. Thus a South Carolina court held that a school could not make a blanket rule banning all demonstrations on school property without regard to how orderly and peaceful they were. The court stated that under the First Amendment the school campus was a proper place for students to assemble for "peaceful expression of grievances" against school policies. [28]

In another case, a federal court in Puerto Rico held that a school rule prohibiting off-campus demonstrations that "affected the institutional order" was too vague and overbroad to be constitutional. [29] The court said that school officials would have to make more specific rules describing the type of conduct that would be considered to affect the order of the school before they could constitutionally enforce such a rule.

From these cases it is clear that demonstrations during school hours run a greater risk of being held illegal than those held after school, for two reasons: (1) they are more likely to disrupt classes, and (2) many of the demonstrators will be illegally absent from classes. It goes without saying that your participation in any demonstration off campus, after school hours, is of no concern to school authorities. [30]

If you take part in a demonstration during school hours, miss classes, and consequently have your grades lowered, you might find out if other students who are truant generally suffer any penalty. If you are treated differently merely because your truancy resulted from a demonstration, the punishment may be illegal.

One final word: Whether your demonstration is inside a building or out on the campus, a court is more likely to find the action legal if it concerns school policies rather than non-school issues. While a court may not be persuaded that a school is the proper place to protest against United States foreign policy, it might recognize that it is the only effective place to protest against a long-hair regulation. In the words of the Supreme Court, "We would be ignoring reality if we did not recognize that the public schools in a community are important institutions and are often the focus of significant grievances."[31] You should be warned, however, that anyone who demonstrates on school property runs some risk of being arrested.

Can a school prohibit students from handing out all literature, including underground newspapers, on school property?

No. This would violate the Supreme Court's decision in *Tinker*. Literature may be barred from school property only if its distribution materially and substantially interferes with school activities, [32] and even some disruption in handing out the literature does not justify banning the literature completely. As one court said of students in a particular case, "It is their misconduct in the manner in which they distributed the paper which should have been stopped, not the idea of printing newspapers itself."[33]

That same court emphasized the point that minor disruptions must be tolerated to accommodate the right of students to express their views. Since the "interruption of class periods caused by the 'newspaper' were minor and relatively few in number," the court said, the *Tinker* standard of "material and substantial disruption" had not been met. A word of advice: Although a rule prohibiting all distribution of literature on school property is unconstitutional, you should ask school officials to change the rule before deciding to defy it.

May a school pass a regulation banning distribution of literature that may cause disruptions?

No. The *Tinker* decision's language permitting school officials to limit First Amendment activities that cause material and substantial disruption does not mean that they can pass a general rule prohibiting disruptive literature and then decide later what is disruptive. Any rule concerning the distribution of literature must be very specific in order to comply with the demands of the First Amendment.

One federal court has held that a school rule prohibiting distribution of literature that could "reasonably lead the principal to forecast substantial disruption of or material interference with school activities" was overly vague.[34] The court recognized that the rule used the *Tinker* language but held that, nevertheless, "a crucial flaw exists in this directive since it gives no guidance whatsoever as to what amounts to a 'substantial disruption of or material interference with school activities'; and equally fatal, it fails to detail the criteria by which an administrator might reasonably predict the occurrence of such a disruption."

On the other hand, courts have permitted school administrators to prohibit distribution of literature in specific emergency situations where imminent violence was reasonably feared. In one case, a federal court upheld the action of school officials in confiscating signs from a student who was distributing them on the day of a planned walkout from a school athletic awards ceremony.[35] The court found that in light of the generally tense atmosphere in the school caused by the announced walkout and rumors that the athletes scheduled to receive the awards planned to stop physically anyone leaving the ceremony, school officials' fear of violence was reasonable and justified the emergency confiscation of the leaflets. The court went on to hold, however, that while the emergency justified the confiscation of the literature, the suspension of the student for distributing leaflets violated his First Amendment rights.

Can students express their views by handing out leaflets in a classroom or in the halls or by setting up a literature table in the lobby?

Sometimes. Although the Supreme Court did not consider these specific means of expression in *Tinker*, it did establish the "material and substantial disruption" standard by which you should be able to determine whether your activities are protected by the First Amendment.

The words "material" and "substantial" are crucial because the Court recognized that *any* expression of opinion on a controversial issue may upset some people. In the Court's own words, "Any word spoken, in class, in the lunchroom, or on the campus, that deviates from the views of another person may start an argument or cause a disturbance." Such a minor disturbance or disruption, however, is no justification for prohibiting students from expressing their views.

Now, apply that reasoning to the examples in the question:

1. *Leaflets in the classroom.* Certainly this is not legally protected while class is in session and perhaps not before class either, since this activity might interfere with students' getting to their seats and preparing for class.

2. *Leaflets in the halls.* Although this would not directly interfere with classes, you might substantially interfere with traffic in the halls and delay students from getting to class on time, especially in schools with narrow, crowded halls. A court applying the *Tinker* test might, therefore, find such methods of distribution to be illegal. On the other hand, a blanket rule against handing out literature anywhere inside a school has been declared illegal by some courts, although school officials may make reasonable rules regarding the time and place of distribution.[36] However, a rule restricting distribution to a time

and place that would prevent most students from getting the literature would not be reasonable. As one court said: "[B]y excluding the period when the vast majority of the desired audience will be present and available for communication, the restriction is in effect a prohibition. The First Amendment includes the right to receive as well as to disseminate information."[37]

3. *Setting up a literature table in the lobby.* If it's a small lobby and the table or students gathering around it clog up the lobby, you'd have the same problem as with the corridors. On the other hand, if it's a large lobby and there is no substantial interference with students' passing through, and if you are not supposed to be in class or study period, a court would be likely to find that you had a right to set up the table. Your case would be stronger if you were able to show that tables were made available there for, say, the student government to sell prom tickets or the parent-teacher association to have a bake sale. After all, if their tables are not substantially disruptive, yours should not be either.

If a school official tries to stop you because students who take your literature are discarding it on the floor, you might suggest that he instead punish those persons for littering. That is how the law works when leaflets are being passed out in the street.[38] You should point out that if the school stopped you from handing out literature because other students threw it on the floor, it would be easy for those who disagree with you to take your literature and litter the school, and thus defeat your right to express your views.

May a school ban all literature on a given issue as long as the ban applies to all sides?

Some school boards seem to think that students may be prohibited from expressing their views on controversial issues as long as "both sides" are banned. Whether or not such policies are well intentioned, the *Tinker* decision no longer permits school officials to silence students because of the fear that controversy will disrupt the education process. It is, in fact, the discussion of controversial issues, the Supreme Court said, which "is the basis of our national strength and of the independence and vigor of Americans who grow up and live in this relatively permissive, often disputatious society."[39]

One school district barred a student from handing out and posting leaflets seeking volunteers for the "McGovern for President" campaign in 1972, claiming it had a policy prohibiting the use of school facilities for all partisan political activities, including activities on behalf of both major political parties. Nevertheless, a federal court ruled that this policy violated the student's First Amendment rights.[40] And another federal court declared unconstitutional a state law prohibiting distribution on school property of any material of a "sectarian, partisan or denominational character" or the purpose of which was to "spread propaganda."[41]

Still another federal court struck down a school regulation prohibiting recruitment among the school population by any organization of "political-partisan and/or religious-sectarian character within the school."[42]

Can a principal require students to submit all literature to him or her for approval in advance of distribution?

No, unless there are clearly defined rules that describe the procedures by which prior approval must be obtained. Two federal appeals courts have even held that no prior approval at all can be required since such a rule would violate the First Amendment prohibition of censorship.[43] Courts that have allowed the requirement of prior approval of literature have demanded that the school board adopt specific procedural rules, such as one clearly stating which literature has to be submitted and to whom it has to be submitted.[44]

Most importantly, if prior approval is required, the school must set a definite and brief time within which a decision has to be made, so that the principal cannot indefinitely delay the distribution. A federal court in California, although approving in theory a policy requiring prior approval of literature, emphasized the need for a quick decision, warning that where the literature is "political or social, and the effectiveness of the item may be severely diminished by even a brief delay in its distribution, it may be that even one day's restraint is an impermissible burden."[45] If, for example, you have to submit to the dean for his or her approval a leaflet announcing a rally the next afternoon, you have a very strong argument for requesting a decision the same day.

Finally, the school may be required to provide an opportunity for the students to present their point of view at a hearing. If a decision disapproving their literature is made, students must have available to them "an expeditious review procedure of the decision of school authorities."[46]

It should be obvious, of course, in view of *Tinker*, that the school may not withhold approval of literature without evidence that its distribution will materially and substantially disrupt the school. Even without court orders, such large urban school districts as Philadelphia and New York City have decided on their own that it would not be proper to require students to submit literature for advance approval.[47] This policy is better because, among other reasons, it preserves the students' anonymity and thus prevents school officials from punishing those who distribute controversial literature.

Can students *sell* literature on school grounds as long as there is no substantial disruption of school activities?

Courts have disagreed on this issue. One federal court has ruled that students could not be barred from selling literature or soliciting advertising for it unless under the *Tinker* test there was evidence of disruption.[48] But a second court upheld a prohibition against selling any product, including political literature, on school property.[49] Even under that court's holding, which we believe to be inconsistent with the reasoning of *Tinker*, it would be illegal to prohibit the sale of your literature if the sale of other student literature, such as the school newspaper, is permitted.

Another court held that a school regulation prohibiting dissemination of commercial advertisements and solicitation of funds could not lawfully be applied to an underground newspaper that accepted commercial advertising and solicited donations to support itself.[50] The court, pointing out that the school subscribed to many magazines containing ads, found that "the dissemination of commercial advertisements and solicitation of funds within a publication devoted largely to expression of opinion and factual matter can scarcely be said to be an evil which, standing by itself, is in need of elimination." In two other cases where courts broadly upheld the right to distribute underground newspapers on school property, the papers were either sold[51] or contributions were solicited.[52]

Can students solicit money on school grounds to support political and social causes?

Raising money to support causes in which one believes has long been held to be a protected activity under the First Amendment;[53] therefore, the *Tinker* test of material and substantial disruption ought to apply to this kind of activity. The one court that directly considered the issue, however, denied students the right to distribute flyers soliciting funds for the defense of a political trial; the court feared that students might be subjected to pressure by various outside groups seeking to raise money for particular causes.[54]

If you want to solicit money in your school for a political or social cause, you should try to show that no serious problems would arise, such as substantial disruption of school activities or undue pressure being put upon students to contribute. One way you might show this is to give examples of other types of solicitations that are permitted by school authorities, such as various ticket sales, bake sales, sales of school publications, solicitations for charity, raising money for student government, sale of school rings, etc. For example, the New York State Commissioner of Education has permitted a student council to sell candy in order to finance student activities.[55] If money may be solicited for these purposes, it is unfair, and perhaps illegal, to prohibit students from soliciting money for other purposes.

May a student publication be banned because it criticizes a school rule and advises students to disobey it?

Once again, the starting point is the *Tinker* test of material and substantial disruption. To bar such a publication, school officials would have to be able to show that its distribution on school property would be likely to produce some serious disorder at the school.

In the major case on this question, students in an Illinois high school produced a newspaper urging their classmates to throw away some materials that were given them by the school staff to take to their parents. A federal appeals court said that the publication was protected by the First Amendment since there was no evidence from which school officials could reasonably have forecast a substantial disruption of school activity.[56] In other words, the students were not rallying their classmates and preparing them for immediate action to disrupt the school.

Two other federal courts have taken the same position. One declared invalid a school regulation prohibiting any publication that advocates illegal action or disobedience to published rules on student conduct.[57] The other found unconstitutional a school board policy prohibiting distribution of any publication which "advocates illegal actions, or is grossly insulting to any group or individual."[58]

Can a publication be banned because it criticizes school officials?

No. Criticism of school policies and school officials is protected by the First Amendment. Some principals say that published criticism of school staff will undermine discipline among students. However, courts have not permitted such criticism to be suppressed if the school officials were unable to produce specific evidence that discipline would be substantially affected by the publication's distribution. One student publication suggested that a dean had a "sick mind," a remark that a court found "disrespectful and tasteless," but not justifying suppression of the publication under the *Tinker* test.[60]

Sometimes a school official will try to ban a critical article or publication because it is libelous. Libel is printing something that you know, or should know, is not true in an attempt to injure a person's reputation. If what you write is libelous, you can be sued for money damages. If your criticism concerns school policies, and you have good reason to believe that what you say is true, the statements will not constitute libel even if you are not able to prove they are true or even if what you write later turns out to be false. Nothing you say that is true is libelous.

This standard has been specifically enunciated by the Supreme Court in a number of cases not involving students. At least one federal court has struck down a school rule prohibiting the publication of "libelous" material in a school newspaper where the definition of libel used by the school was different from that of the Supreme Court.[61]

If the school pays for a student-run publication, do school officials have total control over its contents?

No. Even though the school pays for the publication, school officials may not act as a censor of its contents if it has been a forum for the expression of student views. They may not prevent the publication of an article or editorial merely because it is critical of school policies or because they consider it too controversial.[62] In the words of one court, "The state is not necessarily the unfettered master of all it creates."[63]

This rule has been applied to a case where students attempted to place an antiwar advertisement in the school newspaper. Although the newspaper accepted commercial advertisements, the principal refused to permit publication of the ad because it did not relate to news of the high school. The court rejected this argument, noting that articles on the war had appeared in the paper and that the war was clearly a school-related issue.[64] Of significance is the fact that the court did not deny students this forum for communicating their views even though other modes of expression—such as conversation or armbands—existed for the students.

In other cases, courts have barred school officials from cutting off funds to campus newspapers because they disapproved of the newspapers' content.[65]

In a case involving university students, a federal court upheld a lower court decision enjoining university officials from banning a student literary magazine of which it disapproved. The court held that the fact that the magazine was required to be published with help from the university's English department did not entitle the university to censor its contents on the theory that the magazine would be identified as speaking for the English department. On appeal, over the objection of the students, the court hit upon the compromise of allowing the university to stamp on the cover a disclaimer stating that the magazine was not an official publication of the university.[66]

Similar First Amendment principles were applied to an official student yearbook. Graduating seniors had traditionally been permitted to print a quotation of their choice next to their pictures. One student who wished to express her feelings about capital punishment submitted a quotation from a magazine that graphically described the effects on the body of electrocution. School officials thought the quote was "inappropriate" and "in poor taste" and prohibited the student from using it. A federal court held the prohibition unconstitutional.[67]

A word of caution. As this book went to press, the Supreme Court was reviewing a case involving articles printed in a school newspaper produced by a journalism class. One article discussed three students' experiences with pregnancy, and a second article addressed the impact of divorce on children. The Court's holding in this case may substantially alter what has been said here about school-sponsored publications[68]

May school officials remove books from school libraries because they disapprove of the ideas those books express?

No. The Supreme Court in the *Island Trees* case[69] held that a school library provides an "environment especially appropriate for the recognition of the First Amendment rights of students." In that case, a school board had ordered the removal of nine books from school libraries on the ground that the books were contrary to the values of the school board members and the community they represented. The Court conceded that school officials have "significant discretion to determine the content of their school libraries. But that discretion," the Court held, "may not be exercised in a narrowly partisan or political manner." Thus, school officials "may not remove books from school library shelves simply because they dislike the ideas contained in those books. . . ."

One court has applied the principles of the *Island Trees* decision to an attempt by school officials to bar a grade school class from performing a play that expressed ideas of which they disapproved.[70] The court noted that participation in the play was voluntary and that the play was not part of the school's curriculum, over which school officials would have greater discretion. Based on its finding that the school board had "ordered a halt to production solely because it did not approve of the content of the play," the court held that the board and its members acted unconstitutionally. Quoting one of the justices in the *Island Trees* case, the court said that "allowing a school board to engage in such conduct hardly teaches children to respect the diversity of ideas that is fundamental to the American system."

Can student literature or other forms of speech be prohibited because school officials find them vulgar and indecent?

A recent Supreme Court decision makes clear that school officials have substantial power to prohibit student speech that they consider to be vulgar or indecent. Although the extent of that power is uncertain, you will avoid trouble if you can avoid using so-called "dirty words" and sexual references in what you write and say.

In the Supreme Court case *Bethel School District No. 403 v. Fraser*,[71] the Court upheld the suspension of a student who had delivered a speech before a school assembly nominating a fellow student for a school elected office. The speech, which was characterized by the Supreme Court as "an elaborate, graphic, and explicit sexual metaphor," went as follows:

I know a man who is firm—he's firm in his pants, he's firm in his shirt, his character is firm—but most . . . of all, his belief in you, the students of Bethel, is firm.

Jeff Kuhlman is a man who takes his point and pounds it in. If necessary, he'll take an issue and nail it to the wall. He doesn't attack things in spurts—he drives hard, pushing and pushing until finally—he succeeds.

Jeff is a man who will go to the very end—even the climax, for each and every one of you.

So vote for Jeff for A.S.B. vice-president—he'll never come between you and the best our high school can be.

In holding that the speech was not constitutionally protected, the Court observed that schools have an "interest in teaching students the boundaries of socially appropriate behavior" and that it was, therefore, "a highly appropriate function of public school education to prohibit the use of vulgar and offensive terms in public discourse." While this reasoning may suggest that school officials have unlimited power to censor student speech that they believe is vulgar and tasteless, the facts in the *Bethel* case on which the Supreme Court rendered its decision make it likely that the effect of the ruling will not be so broad. The Court noted, among other things, that the student had discussed his speech with two teachers who had specifically informed him that the speech was "inappropriate and that he probably should not deliver it"; the audience at the school assembly consisted of young teenagers, mostly 14-year-olds; and, according to the Court, some students hearing the speech "hooted and yelled; some by gestures graphically simulated the sexual activities pointedly alluded to in [the] speech. Other students appeared to be bewildered and embarrassed by the speech. One teacher reported that on the day following the speech, she found it necessary to forgo a portion of the scheduled class lesson in order to discuss the speech with the class."

Bethel probably will not seriously affect student publications because these rarely will provoke the reaction that the speech did in *Bethel*. There is reason for some hope, therefore, that subsequent court decisions will heed the warning of a respected federal judge that "school officials . . . do [not] have limitless discretion to apply their own notions of indecency. Courts have a First Amendment responsibility to insure that robust rhetoric . . . is not suppressed by prudish failures to distinguish the vigorous from the vulgar."[72]

If you think it necessary to use language that school officials might consider vulgar, or if you wish to distribute an already written article that contains such language, you might try to explain why the particular language is essential to the point you are trying to make. As one federal judge noted, "Critics of the established order have frequently found it necessary to use language that shocked their audiences—neither Ezekiel nor Martin Luther spoke in bland terms."[73] It would also be helpful to point out that many books and articles in the school library contain the same words to which the principal is objecting in the student literature.[74] One court, faced with such a situation, attacked the school officials for their "rank inconsistency," which the court found "arbitrary and unreasonable."[75]

A federal court in New York, in a case involving the censorship of a student publication because a story contained "four-letter words as part of the vocabulary of an adolescent and . . . a description of a movie scene where a couple 'fell into bed,' " held that "constitutionally permissible censorship based on obscenity must be premised on a rational finding of harmfulness to the group [to whom the material is directed or from whom it is withheld]."[76] The dialogue was the kind "heard repeatedly by those who walk the streets of our cities, use public conveyances and deal with youth in an open manner." Because similar language appears in reputable books and magazines readily available to students, the language in the story could not be considered offensive to community standards for minors and therefore should not have been censored.

Can students remain quietly seated during the flag salute

ceremony as a symbolic protest against the words of the Pledge
of Allegiance?

Yes. On the basis of the principles we have discussed, namely
that peaceful and orderly protest is permissible if it does not
substantially disrupt school activities, every reported court decision on this issue has permitted students to remain quietly
seated during the flag salute to symbolize their disagreement
with the nation's policies or practices. The major Supreme
Court case dealing with the flag salute was *West Virginia State
Board of Education v. Barnette*,[77] in which Jehovah's Witnesses
won the right to refuse to salute the flag. Although the claim
in that case was for religious freedom, the Court made clear
that a compulsory flag salute violated the right of all citizens
to free expression,[78] quite apart from their religious convictions.[79]

The further question of the right to remain seated during
the flag salute was raised by students in New York City, who
felt that the words to the Pledge of Allegiance were not true
in America today.[80] The school argued that other students had
followed the example of the original students and were remaining seated, a consequence which the court did not find
disturbing: "The First Amendment protects successful dissent
as well as ineffective protest." As to the fear of school officials
that other students might become "infuriated" at those who
sat, the court said, "The Constitution does not recognize fears
of a disorderly reaction as ground for restricting peaceful
expression." The court held that, under the *Tinker* test, students had the right to remain quietly seated during the flag
salute as a matter of conscience.

The next year, when some students in one of the same schools
found themselves being harassed for remaining seated, the
court issued a further order stating that the students could not
be required to obtain parental permission in order to remain
seated.[81]

Three federal courts of appeals have reached similar conclusions and have upheld the rights of students to remain quietly seated during the flag salute.[82]

Do school officials have the right to conduct religious ex-
ercises in school?

No. The Supreme Court has held that school prayers and
ritual Bible readings, ceremonies which many schools hold at

the beginning of classes each day, violate the students' First Amendment right to freedom of religion, even if the prayers are nondenominational and participation is voluntary.[83] Such ceremonies are illegal despite the fact that students may be excused from attending them.[84]

The Supreme Court has also declared unconstitutional the practice of posting the Ten Commandments in classrooms when the purpose of the posting was religious rather than educational.[85] Similarly, a state law mandating a moment of silence at the beginning of the school day, even when participation was not required, was invalidated because the Court found that the primary purpose of the law was to advance religion. The Court expressed a special concern about government endorsed religious activities in schools, even when voluntary, because government endorsement was more likely to result in coerced religious beliefs.[86]

Federal courts have disagreed as to whether or not the recitation of brief prayers at athletic contests or graduation ceremonies was unconstitutional.[87]

A variation of these problems is presented by "released time" programs which allow students to leave school for a period of time during the day for religious instruction. Such programs have been found constitutional by the courts as long as students are not pressured to participate and the educational program of nonparticipating students is not disrupted.[88]

Can a school require a student who has religious objections to participation in war and military training to take part in an ROTC or similar program?

No. A federal court has held that a high school student who, by reason of religious training and belief, was conscientiously opposed to participating in military training could not be compelled, as a prerequisite for a diploma, to participate in a Reserve Officers Training Corps (ROTC) or other such program.[89]

Can student groups meet on school property during noninstructional time for religious purposes?

Yes, as long as other student groups are permitted to hold meetings on school property. The right of student groups to hold meetings for religious purposes during noninstructional time to the same extent that nonreligious student groups may hold meetings is guaranteed by the Equal Access Act.[90] The act imposes some restrictions: the meetings must be student-initiated, they must not be school-sponsored, school staff may attend only in a nonparticipatory capacity; and nonschool persons may not direct, conduct, control, or regularly attend such meetings.

NOTES

1. *Shanley v. Northeast Independent School District*, 462 F.2d 960 (5th Cir. 1972)
2. *Tinker v. Des Moines Independent Community School Dist.*, 393 U.S. 503 (1969).
3. *Butts v. Dallas Independent School District*, 436 F.2d 728 (5th Cir. 1971).
4. *Sullivan v. Houston Independent School District*, 307 F. Supp. 1328 (S.D. Tex. 1969) cert. denied, 414 U.S. 1032 (1973).
5. *Guzick v. Drebus*, 431 F.2d 594 (6th Cir. 1970), *cert. denied*, 401 U.S. 948 (1971).
6. *Shanley v. Northeast Independent School District*, 462 F.2d 960 (5th Cir. 1972).
7. *Butts v. Dallas Independent School District*, 436 F.2d 728 (5th Cir. 1971).
8. *Augustus v. School Board of Escambia County, Fla.*, 361 F. Supp. 383 (N.D. Fla. 1973), *modified and remanded*, 507 F.2d 152 (5th Cir. 1975).
9. *Burnside v. Byars*, 363 F.2d 744 (5th Cir. 1966).
10. *Blackwell v. Issaquena County Board of Education*, 363 F.2d 749 (5th Cir. 1966).
11. *Guzick v. Drebus*, 431 F.2d 594 (6th Cir. 1970), *cert. denied*, 401 U.S. 948 (1971).
12. *Wise v. Sauers*, 345 F. Supp. 90 (E.D. Pa. 1972) aff'd. by 481 F. 2d 1400 (1973).
13. *Bonner-Lyons v. School Committee of Boston*, 480 F.2d 442 (1st Cir. 1973). See also *National Socialist White People's Party v. Ringers*, 473 F.2d 1010 (4th Cir. 1973); *Zucker v. Panitz*, 299 F. Supp. 102 (S.D.N.Y. 1969); *Garvin v. Rosenau*, 455 F.2d 233 (6th Cir. 1972), *on remand*, Civil Action No. 36093 (E.D. Mich. 1972); *A.C.L.U. v. Radford College*, 315 F. Supp. 893 (W.D. Va. 1970).
14. *Clergy and Laity Concerned v. Chicago Board of Education*, 586 F. Supp. 1408 (N.D. Ill. 1984).

15. 20 U.S.C. §4071 *et seq.*

16. *Student Coalition for Peace v. Lower Merion School District*, 776 F.2d 431 (3d Cir. 1985).

17. *N.A.A.C.P. v. Button*, 371 U.S. 415 (1963).

18. *Garvin v. Rosenau*, 455 F.2d 233 (6th Cir. 1972), *on remand,* Civil Action No. 36093 (E.D. Mich. 1972).

19. *Healy v. James*, 408 U.S. 169 (1972).

20. *Dixon v. Beresh*, 361 F. Supp. 253 (E.D. Mich. 1973).

21. *Gay Alliance of Students v. Matthews*, 544 F.2d 162 (4th Cir. 1976).

22. *Gay Students Organization of Univ. of New Hampshire v. Bonner*, 509 F.2d 652 (1st Cir. 1974).

23. *Molpus v. Fortune*, 432 F.2d 916 (5th Cir. 1970); *Vail v. Board of Education of Portsmouth School District*, 354 F. Supp. 592 (D.N.H. 1973).

24. *Tate v. Board of Education of the Jonesboro (Arkansas) Special School District*, 453 F.2d 975 (8th Cir. 1972).

25. *Dunn v. Tyler Independent School District*, 460 F.2d 137 (5th Cir. 1972).

26. *Sword v. Fox*, 446 F.2d 1091 (4th Cir. 1971).

27. *Gebert v. Hoffman*, 336 F. Supp. 694 (E.D. Pa. 1972). See also *Jenkins v. Louisiana State Board of Education*, 506 F.2d 992 (5th Cir. 1975).

28. *Hammond v. South Carolina State College*, 272 F. Supp. 947 (D. S.C. 1967).

29. *Cintron v. State Board of Education*, 384 F. Supp. 674 (D.P.R. 1974).

30. *Shanley v. Northeast Independent School District*, 462 F.2d 960 (5th Cir. 1972).

31. *Grayned v. City of Rockford*, 408 U.S. 104 (1972).

32. *Eisner v. Stamford Board of Education*, 440 F.2d 803 (2d Cir. 1971); *Quarterman v. Byrd*, 453 F.2d 54 (4th Cir. 1971); *Shanley v. Northeast Independent School District*, 462 F.2d 960 (5th Cir. 1972); *Scoville v. Board of Education of Joliet Township*, 425 F.2d 10 (7th Cir. 1970).

33. *Sullivan v. Houston Independent School District*, 307 F. Supp. 1328 (S.D. Tex. 1969).

34. *Nitzberg v. Parks*, 525 F.2d 378 (4th Cir. 1975).

35. *Karp v. Becken*, 477 F.2d 171 (9th Cir. 1973).

36. *Riseman v. School Committee of Quincy*, 439 F.2d 148 (1st Cir. 1971); *Sullivan v. Houston Independent School District*, 307 F. Supp. 1328 (S.D. Tex. 1969) cert. denied, 414 U.S. 1032 (1973). *Hilly v. Cunningham*, Civil Action No. 70-1528-C (D. Mass. 11/12/70).

37. *Rowe v. Campbell Union High School District*, Civil Action No. 51060 (N.D. Calif. 9/4/70) (3-judge court).

38. *Id.* See also *Schneider v. New Jersey*, 308 U.S. 147 (1939).

39. *Tinker v. Des Moines Independent School District*, 393 U.S. 503 (1969).

40. *Sanders v. Martin*, 72C 1398 (E.D.N.Y. 11/21/72).

41. *Rowe v. Campbell Union High School District*, Civil Action No. 51060 (N.D. Calif. 9/4/70) (3-judge court).

42. *Cintron v. State Board of Education*, 384 F. Supp. 674 (D.P.R. 1974).

43. *Riseman v. School Committee of Quincy*, 439 F.2d 148 (1st Cir. 1971); *Fujishima v. Board of Education*, 460 F.2d 1355 (7th Cir. 1972). See also *Poxon v. Board of Education*, Civil Action No. S1894 (E.D. Calif. 8/31/71).

44. *Eisner v. Stamford Board of Education*, 440 F.2d 803 (2d Cir. 1971); *Shanley v. Northeast Independent School District*, 462 F.2d 960 (5th Cir. 1972); *Quarterman v. Byrd*, 453 F.2d 54 (4th Cir. 1971).

45. *Rowe v. Campbell Union High School District*, Civil Action No. 51060 (N.D. Calif. 1971) (3-judge court).

46. *Shanley v. Northeast Independent School District*, 462 F.2d 960 (5th Cir. 1972).

47. Both school districts' policies are cited in *Sullivan v. Houston Independent School District*, 307 F. Supp. 1328 (S.D. Tex. 1969). See also *Matter of Williams*, decision of the New York City Board of Education (3/30/71).

48. *Pliscou v. Holtville Unified School District.*, 411 F. Supp. 842 (S.D. Calif. 1976).

49. *Glover v. Cole*, 762 F.2d 1197 (4th Cir. 1985).

50. *Peterson v. Board of Education of School District No. 1 of Lincoln, Neb.*, 370 F. Supp. 1208 (D. Neb. 1973).

51. *Scoville v. Board of Education of Joliet Township*, 425 F.2d 10 (7th Cir. 1970).

52. *Sullivan v. Houston Independent School District*, 307 F. Supp. 1328 (S.D. Tex. 1969). In addition, the Commissioner of Education of New Jersey upheld the right of students to sell a newspaper inside the school building. *Burke v. Board of Education of Township of Livingston*, N.J. 1970 School Law Dec. 319.

53. *Murdock v. Pennsylvania*, 319 U.S. 105 (1943).

54. *Katz v. McAulay*, 438 F.2d 1058 (2d Cir. 1971).

55. *Matter of Darrall*, 5 Ed. Dept. Rep. 197 (1966).

56. *Scoville v. Board of Education of Joliet Township*, 425 F.2d 10 (7th Cir. 1970).

57. *Molpus v. Fortune*, 432 F.2d 916 (5th Cir. 1970). See also *Matter of Brociner*, 11 Ed. Dept. Rep. 204 (New York State Commissioner of Education 1972).

58. *Baughman v. Freienmuth*, 478 F.2d 1345 (4th Cir. 1973).

59. *Cintron v. State Board of Education*, 384 F. Supp. 674 (D. P.R. 1974).

60. *Scoville v. Board of Education of Joliet Township*, 425 F.2d 10 (7th Cir. 1970).

61. *Nitzberg v. Parks*, 525 F.2d 378 (4th Cir. 1975).

62. *Trujillo v. Love*, 322 F. Supp. 1266 (D. Colo. 1971); *Antonelli v. Hammond*, 308 F. Supp. 1329 (D. Mass. 1970).

63. *Trujillo v. Love*, 322 F. Supp. 1266 (D. Colo. 1971). See also *Wesolek v. The Board of Trustees South Bend Community School Corp.*, Civil Action No. 73 S 101 (S.D. Ind. 5/25/73).

64. *Zucker v. Panitz*, 299 F. Supp. 102 (S.D.N.Y. 1969). See also *San Diego Committee Against Registration and the Draft (CARD) v. Governing Board of Grossmont Union High School District*, 790 F.2d 1471 (9th Cir. 1986). (Antidraft protesters cannot be barred from placing ads in school newspapers when military recruiting ads are accepted.)

65. *Joyner v. Whiting*, 477 F.2d 456 (4th Cir. 1973); *Stanley v. Magrath*, 719 F.2d 279 (8th Cir. 1983).

66. *Bazaar v. Fortune*, 476 F.2d 570 (5th Cir. 1973), *aff'd as modified*, 489 F.2d 225 (5th Cir. 1973).

67. *Stanton v. Brunswick School Dept.*, 577 F. Supp. 1560 (D. Maine 1984).

68. *Hazelwood School District v. Kuhlmeier, cert. granted*, 55 *U.S. Law Week* 3489 (1/20/87).

69 *Board of Education, Island Trees Union Free School District No. 26 v. Pico*, 457 U.S. 853 (1982).

70. *Bowman v. Bethel-Tate Board of Education*, 610 F. Supp. 577 (D. Ohio 1985).

71. *Bethel School District No. 403 v. Fraser*, 106 S.Ct. 3159 (1986).

72. *Thomas v. Board of Education, Granville Central School District*, 607 F.2d 1043, 1057 (2d Cir. 1979) (Newman, J., concurring).

73. *United States v. Head*, 317 F. Supp. 1138 (E.D. La. 1970).

74. *Board of Education, Island Trees Union Free School District No. 26 v. Pico*, 457 U.S. 853 (1982); *Keefe v. Geanakos*, 418 F.2d 359 (1st Cir. 1969).

75. *Vought v. Van Buren Public Schools*, 306 F. Supp. 1388 (E.D. Mich. 1969).

76. *Kopell v. Levine*, 347 F. Supp. 456 (E.D.N.Y 1972). See also *Jacobs*

v. Board of School Commissioners of Indianapolis, 349 F. Supp. 605 (S.D. Ind. 1972), *aff'd*, 490 F.2d 601 (7th Cir. 1973), *vacated as moot*, 420 U.S. 128 (1975).

77. *West Virginia State Board of Education v. Barnette*, 319 U.S. 624 (1943).
78. *Street v. New York*, 394 U.S. 576 (1969).
79. *State of Maryland v. Lundquist*, 278 A.2d 263 (Ct. App. Md. 1971).
80. *Frain v. Baron*, 307 F. Supp. 27 (E.D.N.Y. 1969).
81. The New York State Commissioner of Education has made the same ruling. *Matter of Bustin*, 10 Ed. Dept. Rep. 168 (1971).
82. *Banks v. Board of Public Instruction*, 314 F. Supp. 285 (S.D. Fla.), *aff'd*, 450 F.2d 1103 (5th Cir. 1971); *Goetz v. Ansell*, 477 F.2d 636 (2d Cir. 1973); *Lipp v. Morris*, 579 F.2d 834 (3d Cir. 1978).
83. *Engel v. Vitale*, 370 U.S. 421 (1962).
84. *Murray v. Curlett*, 374 U.S. 203 (1963).
85. *Stone v. Graham*, 449 U.S. 39 (1980).
86. *Wallace v. Jaffree*, 472 U.S. 38 (1985).
87. Compare *Graham v. Central Community School District of Decatur County*, 608 F. Supp. 531 (D. Iowa 1985) with *Stein v. Plainwell Community Schools*, 610 F. Supp. 43 (D. Mich. 1985).
88. *Zorach v. Clauson*, 343 U.S. 306 (1952).
89. *Spence v. Bailey*, 465 F.2d 797 (6th Cir. 1972).
90. 20 U.S.C. §4071 *et seq.*

Addendum to Chapter Two

Supreme Court Says School Officials Have Right to Censor Official School Newspaper

As this book went to press, the United States Supreme Court, in *Hazelwood School District v. Kuhlmeier* (decided January 15, 1988), upheld the power of school officials to control the content of school-financed newspapers. The Court's decision overturned the long-standing view of nearly all lower federal courts that the content of official school newspapers should be determined by student editors, whose judgment could be overruled by school officials only if, under the *Tinker* standard, a story threatened to substantially or materially disrupt the educational process.

As a result of the *Kuhlmeier* decision, school officials now may censor stories in official school publications so long as, in the words of the Supreme Court, "their actions are reasonably related to legitimate pedagogical concerns." According to the Court, one appropriate concern of school officials is that readers "are not exposed to material that may be inappropriate for their level of maturity." In the *Kuhlmeier* case, one of the censored articles was about students' experiences with pregnancy. The school principal said that the article's references to sexual activity and birth control were inappropriate for some of the younger students at the school.

To avoid censorship of such potentially controversial subjects, editors should make an effort to show that students are already exposed to these topics in places such as school library books, local newspapers, rap groups, counseling programs, or other programs or activities in which teenagers in that community engage. If editors can show that such subjects are generally considered suitable for high school students in other situations, a principal would have less basis for censoring an article on the ground that its subject is unsuitable. If the principal continues to insist on censorship, editors may be able to demonstrate that it is the article's *point of view*, rather than its subject matter, that concerns the principal. Nothing that the Supreme Court said in the *Kuhlmeier* decision gives a principal the right to censor an article because of disagreement with its point of view.

The Court's decision distinguished between student speech

that is part of the school curriculum, such as official publications, theatrical productions, and other school-sponsored activities, and all other forms of student speech that take place on school property. The latter would include leaflets, buttons, unofficial, or so-called underground, newspapers, and other literature that is not school financed. As to all such forms of speech, the *Tinker* standards discussed throughout this chapter continue to apply. In other words, *Kuhlmeier* gives school officials no greater power to control either the content or form of such student speech than they had previously. Thus, school officials may *not* censor such speech merely because they believe it to be biased, poorly written, vulgar, or unsuitable for immature students. Speech that is not part of the school curriculum may be prohibited only if there is evidence that it will materially and substantially disrupt the work of the school.

III

Personal Appearance

Do schools have the right to regulate students' personal appearance?

The Supreme Court's ruling in *Tinker* upheld the right of students to wear buttons and other symbols of their political viewpoints on the ground that this is a constitutionally protected interest falling under the right of free expression. A student's personal appearance, however, is a somewhat different matter. Although the way one looks and dresses is a fundamental form of personal expression and should, therefore, be protected by the constitutional guarantees of privacy and free speech, not all courts have agreed that students are free to dress and groom themselves as they please. Even courts that have held that the Constitution prohibits school officials from arbitrarily regulating students' personal appearance have, nevertheless, balanced the rights of the student against the need of the school to make reasonable health and safety regulations.

Can schools regulate the style of a student's hair?

Given the hairstyles popular among young people at the end of the 1980s, it seems virtually unbelievable that a burning issue in the federal courts a mere 15 years ago was whether school officials could force young men with below-collar-length hair to cut it. But in fact, countless hours of litigation would have been spared had only school officials throughout the nation had the wisdom of one Boston federal court judge who wrote:

> This Court takes judicial notice that hairstyles have altered from time to time throughout the ages. Samson's locks symbolically signified his virility. Many of the Founding Fathers of this country wore wigs. President Lincoln grew a beard at the suggestion of a juvenile female admirer. Chief Justice Hughes' beard furnished the model for the frieze over the portico of the Supreme Court of the United States proclaiming "equal justice under law." Today many of both the younger and the older generations have avoided the increased cost of barbering by allowing their locks or

burnsides to grow to greater lengths than when a haircut
cost a quarter of a dollar.

Whether hairstyles be regarded as evidence of conformity or of individuality, they are one of the most visible
examples of personality. This is what every woman has
always known. And so have many men, without the aid
of an anthropologist, behavioral scientist, psychiatrist, or
practitioner of any of the fine arts or black arts.[1]

Nevertheless, the law developed in the long-hair days still
applies to mohawks and spikes, confusing and contradictory
though that law is.

The federal courts are, in fact, split down the middle on the
question of hair regulations in public schools. Some recognize
that students have a constitutional right to determine their own
hairstyle and have held that schools may not regulate the style
of a student's hair unless they can show either a rational relationship between the rule and a legitimate educational purpose or that hair length causes substantial disruption of school
activities. States governed by these decisions include:

Arkansas, Connecticut, Idaho, Illinois, Indiana, Iowa,
Maine, Massachusetts, Minnesota, Missouri, Nebraska,
New Hampshire, New Jersey, New York, North Carolina,
North Dakota, Rhode Island, South Carolina, South Da-
kota, Vermont, Virginia, West Virginia, and Wisconsin.

In addition, some states' education departments have simply
adopted sensible hair regulations. In Pennsylvania, for example, the rule is: "Students have the right to govern the length
or style of their hair including facial hair. Any limitation of this
right shall include evidence that the length or style of hair
causes a disruption of the educational process or constitutes a
health or safety hazard. Where length or style of the hair presents a problem some types of covering should be considered."[2]

Other courts have held that schools are free to regulate
students' hairstyles without having to justify such rules with a
sound educational reason. States governed by these decisions
include:

Alabama, Alaska, Arizona, California, Colorado, Florida,
Georgia, Hawaii, Kansas, Kentucky, Louisiana, Michigan,

Mississippi, Montana, Nevada, New Mexico, Ohio, Oklahoma, Oregon, Tennessee, Texas, Utah, Washington, and Wyoming.

One court in this group held, for example, that although at the public college level, hairstyle regulations cannot, absent exceptional circumstances, be justified by the school's asserted educational and disciplinary needs, in the public elementary and secondary schools such regulations are always justified by the school's needs. This court was willing simply to presume that hairstyle regulations are "a reasonable means of furthering the school board's undeniable interest in teaching hygiene, instilling discipline, asserting authority, and compelling uniformity."[3]

It should be understood that courts having jurisdiction over the *second* group of states have not *required* schools to regulate the style of a student's hair. All they have said is that students have no constitutional right to wear their hair as they please and, therefore, the matter should be left up to the school administrators to make whatever rules they deem necessary. Also, even in these states hairstyle rules are not valid if students do not have fair notice of them[4] or if they exceed the authority local school boards have given to the school to make such rules.[5]

If you live in one of these states, you may still be able to convince your school to abandon hair regulations. Washington, for example, is a state in which hairstyle regulations are permitted; yet the Seattle school district rule on personal appearance is simply that a student's dress or hairstyle must pose no health or safety violation and must not be disruptive.

The reasons most commonly advanced by school officials for regulating hair length are that long hair is distracting in class to other students; that students with long hair tend to be discipline problems and get lower grades than short-haired students; that other students will assault long-haired students; that long hair is unsanitary; that long hair is unsafe in shop classes; and that students must learn to obey rules simply because they are rules.

All of these contentions have been refuted by various courts:

Distraction. A Texas court, considering the distraction argument, asked: "[A]re we really to believe that the appearance of a few long-haired males will topple the pillars of the educational structure of our public schools? If so, then fragile indeed is that structure."[6]

Another court stated that it had "the inescapable feeling that long hair is simply not a source of significant distraction and that school officials are often acting on the basis of personal distaste, amplified by an overzealous belief in the need for the regulations."[7]

Grades. The connection between hair and grades was disputed by one federal court of appeals in these words:

> The connection between long hair and the immemorial problems of misdirected student activism and negativism, whether in behavior or in learning, is difficult to see. No evidence has been presented that hair is the cause, as distinguished from a possible peripheral consequence, of undesirable traits, or that the school board, Delilah-like, can lop off these characteristics with the locks. Accepting as true the testimony that in St. Charles, Missouri, the longer the student's hair, the lower his grade in mathematics, it does not lead me to believe that shortening the one will add to the other. . . .
>
> The area of judicial notice is circumscribed, but I cannot help but observe that the city employee who collects my rubbish has shoulder-length hair. So do a number of our nationally famous Boston Bruins. Barrel tossing and puck chasing are honorable pursuits, not to be associated with effeteness on the one hand, or aimlessness or indolence on the other. If these activities be thought not of high intellectual calibre, I turn to the recent successful candidates for Rhodes Scholarships from my neighboring institution. A number of these, according to their photographs, wear hair that outdoes even the hockey players. It is proverbial that these young men are chosen not only for their scholastic attainments, but for their outstanding character and accomplishments.[8]

Violence. In a widely quoted dissenting opinion, an appeals court judge from Texas rejected the idea that long-haired students could be suspended because other students might attack them: "These boys . . . were barred because it was anticipated that their fellow students in some instances would do things that would disrupt the serenity or calm of the school. It is these acts that should be prohibited, not expressions of individuality by the suspended students."[9]

Sanitation and safety. Sanitation and safety arguments have been easily answered by several courts, which have pointed out that hair length and cleanliness are unrelated and that less drastic alternatives exist to making students get haircuts when long hair might cause a problem, as in a shop class or swimming pool. As one court said, "The school administration has failed to show why these particular problems cannot be solved by imposing less restrictive rules, such as requiring students to wear swimming caps or shop caps."[10]

Respect for rules. As for teaching respect for rules, one court stated: "Discipline for the sake of discipline and uniformity is indeed not compatible with the melting pot formula."[11] Another federal court expressed similar sentiments in holding a school hair regulation unconstitutional: "[T]he constitutional premise is that from different tones comes the best tune."[12]

Is it unlawful sex discrimination for a school to regulate hairstyles only for boys or slacks only for girls?

A case that raised this argument was brought in a district in which hair regulations generally had been found to be constitutionally permissible. The court was not persuaded to change its mind by the boys' argument that they were victims of unlawful sex discrimination since girls were not forced to cut their hair. The court held that the Emergency School Aid Act, which prohibits educational institutions from discriminating on the basis of sex, was not intended to remove all outward differences in the physical appearance of males and females and thus upheld the boys-only long-hair regulation.[13] On similar grounds, a Texas court ruled that the public school hair-length regulation did not violate the equal rights amendment to the state constitution, even though it applied only to males.[14] However, these cases predate the passage of federal regulations to Title IX of the federal Education Amendments of 1972, banning "separate or different rules of behavior, sanctions, or other treatment" on the basis of sex.[15] Students can use these regulations to challenge dress or hair length rules that treat the two sexes differently, even in states where the courts do not recognize a constitutional interest in governing one's own personal appearance.

Can schools regulate what students wear?

Wherever hairstyle can be regulated, dress can be regulated. Where the "disruption" test has been applied to hair regulations, it probably would also apply to dress codes. However, some courts that have permitted students to wear long hair have indicated that a dress code might not be illegal because, unlike hair length, clothes may be changed after school.[16]

Nevertheless, there seems to be no greater reason to regulate dress than hair; dress codes, like hair regulations, generally have more to do with the personal preferences of a school administrator than with education. As one court said in striking down a prohibition against the wearing of dungarees, "[T]he school board's power must be limited to that required by its function of administering public education."[17] The court said it had "difficulty accepting" the proposition advanced by the school principal that students who wore dress such as dungarees "become lax and indifferent."

In an early decision on this question, New York Commissioner of Education James R. Allen, Jr. (later United States Commissioner of Education) ruled that a girl who had worn slacks to school in violation of a school rule could not be barred from school.[18] The commissioner conceded that the board had the power to make reasonable dress regulations relating to health and safety, such as prohibiting the wearing of sweaters in a cooking class; but he held that the regulation against girls wearing slacks was unreasonable and a violation of their constitutional rights.[19] For the same reason, Allen also declared illegal a prohibition against boys wearing boots.[20]

Chancellor's regulations in New York City contain an example of a reasonable dress rule: "Students have the right to determine their own dress, except where such dress is clearly dangerous, or so inappropriate as to interfere with the learning and teaching process."[21]

May students be forced to comply with a dress code or hair regulations adopted by the student body?

Where dress codes and hair regulations have been found illegal when promulgated by the school administration, they have also been found illegal when adopted by the student body.[22] Courts have reasoned that a student's appearance is a matter of personal taste, which should no more be overruled by fellow classmates than by the principal.

Where, however, a dress code promulgated by the school was upheld, a code enacted by the student body was also upheld.[23]

May students be excluded from an athletic team because of the length of their hair?

Unless coaches can show that long hair interferes with athletic performance, there is no more reason to accept regulation of hair length as a condition for playing on a team than as a condition for going to school.[24] Vague fears about threats to discipline and team unity are not enough to justify a hair rule. To quote a New York State Commissioner of Education, neither team morale nor team discipline is "dependent upon uniformity by each member to a given hair style."[25] However, a court in one of the states where schools are free to regulate student hair length ruled that a coach's "clean-shaven" policy for team members was within the school board's power to regulate grooming and was not arbitrary or unreasonable.[26]

May a school require students to wear a special gym outfit?

The right to a free public education guarantees that students do not have to purchase a particular outfit, but a school can require students to wear clothes that permit them to perform the required activities (for example, sneakers) and that are not dangerous (e.g., no jewelry or large belt buckles). Guidelines established by the New York City Board of Education state specifically that schools may recommend but not require the purchase of a gym uniform and that students are to be graded on performance and not dress.[27]

One federal court held that school officials violated the First Amendment by compelling Pentecostal children, over their religious objections, to wear "immodest" gym uniforms.[28]

NOTES

1. *Richards v. Thurston*, 304 F. Supp. 449 (D. Mass. 1969), *aff'd*, 424 F.2d 1281 (1st Cir. 1970); *Mick v. Sullivan*, 476 F.2d 973 (4th Cir. 1973).

2. 22 Pa. Code chap. 12, §12.11(a).

3. *Domico v. Rapides Parish School Board*, 675 F.2d 100 (5th Cir. 1982), *rehearing en banc denied* (6/24/82).

4. *McClung v. Board of Education*, 346 N.E.2d 691 (Ohio Sup. Ct. 1976).

5. *Cordova v. Dhonko*, 315 F. Supp. 953 (N.D. Ohio 1970).

6. *Watson v. Thompson*, 321 F. Supp. 394 (E.D. Tex. 1971).

7. *Breen v. Kahl*, 296 F. Supp. 702 (W.D. Wis.), *aff'd*, 419 F.2d 1034 (7th Cir. 1969), *cert. denied*, 398 U.S. 937 (1970).

8. *Bishop v. Colaw*, 450 F.2d 1069 (8th Cir. 1971).

9. *Ferrell v. Dallas Independent School District*, 392 F.2d 697 (5th Cir. 1968), *cert. denied*, 393 U.S. 856 (1968).

10. *Bishop v. Colaw*, 450 F.2d 1069 (8th Cir. 1971).

11. *Breen v. Kahl*, 296 F. Supp. 702 (W.D. Wis.), *aff'd*, 419 F.2d 1034 (7th Cir. 1969), *cert. denied*, 398 U.S. 937 (1970).

12. *Richards v. Thurston*, 304 F. Supp. 449 (D. Mass. 1969), *aff'd*, 424 F.2d 1281 (1st Cir. 1970); *Massie v. Henry*, 455 F.2d 779 (4th Cir. 1972); *Mick v. Sullivan*, 476 F.2d 973 (4th Cir. 1973).

13. *Trent v. Perritt*, 391 F. Supp. 171 (S.D. Miss. 1975).

14. *Westley v. Rossi*, 305 F. Supp. 706 (D. Minn. 1969).

15. 34 C.F.R. §106.31(b)(4).

16. *Mercer v. Board of Trustees, North Forest Independent School District*, 538 S.W.2d 201 (Civ. App. Tex. 1976).

17. *Dunham v. Pulsifer*, 312 F. Supp. 411 (D. Vt. 1970).

18. *Bannister v. Paradis*, 316 F. Supp. 185 (D.N.H. 1970).

19. *Matter of Dalrymple*, 5 Ed. Dept. Rep. 113 (1966). The same rule was declared invalid by a New York State court: *Scott v. Board of Education, Union Free School District No. 17*, 305 N.Y.S.2d 601 (S. Ct., Nassau Co. 1969).

20. *Matter of McQuade*, 6 Ed. Dept. Rep. 37 (1966).

21. New York City Chancellor's Regulation A- . "Rights and Responsibilities of High School Students," 10/1/79.

22. *Matter of Cossey*, 9 Ed. Dept. Rep. 11 (New York State Commissioner of Education 1969); *Arnold v. Carpenter*, 459 F.2d 939 (7th Cir. 1972); *Bishop v. Colaw*, 450 F.2d 1069 (8th Cir. 1971); *Scott v. Board of Education, Union Free School District No. 17*, 305 N.Y.S.2d 601 (S. Ct., Nassau Co. 1969).

23. *Mercer v. Lothamer*, 321 F. Supp. 335 (N.D. Ohio 1971).

24. *Long v. Zopp*, 476 F.2d 180 (4th Cir. 1973); *Matter of Myers*, 9 Ed. Dept. Rep. 8 (New York State Commissioner of Education 1969); *Dunham v. Pulsifer*, 312 F. Supp. 411 (D. Vt. 1970).

25. *Matter of Vartuli*, 10 Ed. Dept. Rep. 241 (1971).

26. *Davenport by Davenport v. Randolph County Board of Education,*
    730 F.2d 1395 (11th Cir. 1984).
27. New York City Chancellor's Regulation A-540, "Student Dress in
    Physical Education," 10/1/79.
28. *Moody v. Cronin,* 484 F. Supp. 270 (C.D. Ill. 1979).

IV

Discipline and Due Process

Each year more than 1.5 million American students miss a day or more of school because they have been suspended or expelled.[1] The vast majority of these suspensions are not for violent or criminal acts but rather for offenses such as smoking cigarettes or truancy.[2] The National School Boards Association has summarized "what the best research offers" regarding suspension and expulsion:

> Suspended students lose valuable instruction and are likely to distrust the authority that has rejected them.
>
> Minority students are disproportionately suspended and expelled.
>
> Suspension rewards teachers and others for avoiding classroom responsibilities.
>
> Suspended students are usually the very students who most need direct instruction.
>
> Some schools forfeit funds for each suspended or expelled student, under average daily attendance formulas.[3]

The association warns that "traditional approaches—such as punishment, removing troublemakers, and similar measures—often harden delinquent behavior patterns, alienate troubled youths from the schools, and foster distrust."[4]

In recent years, some politicians have called for a return to "good old-fashioned discipline," claiming that due process for students has led to violence and mayhem in the nation's schools. But the author of a study of school safety testified before a congressional committee that not only are educators not unduly fettered but that too many students are suspended. "The real problem," the professor noted, "is the failure of schools to be clear about what their disciplinary procedures are and actually to follow those procedures."[5]

What does the right to "due process of law" mean?

The Constitution requires that government agencies treat all persons fairly. Specifically, the Fourteenth Amendment states that the government may not "deprive any person of life, liberty or property without due process of law." The principal, the teachers, the coaches, the school security guards, and all other employees of the school are employees of the government and therefore under the Fourteenth Amendment have a legal duty to treat you fairly. This means that they may not impose any serious punishment for alleged misconduct without first having followed certain established procedures to determine if you are in fact guilty.

Principals often say that schools are not courtrooms and that school officials must be able to enforce discipline without having to go through all the procedures of a criminal trial. What they ignore is that often the punishments imposed to "enforce discipline" can be as serious as those imposed on a person convicted of a crime. Expulsion from school and the consequent denial of a high school diploma, for example, might have a lifetime effect, depriving a student of a chance to go to college or to obtain many kinds of jobs.

In *Goss v. Lopez*, the Supreme Court held that a "student's legitimate entitlement to a public education [is] a property interest which is protected by the Due Process Clause and . . . may not be taken away for misconduct without adherence to the minimum procedures required by that Clause." The Court went on to say that "the Due Process Clause also forbids arbitrary deprivations of liberty. 'Where a person's good name, reputation, honor or integrity is at stake because of what the government is doing to him,' the minimal requirements of the Clause must be satisfied."[6]

While the *Goss* case is extremely important because it established that a student may not be deprived of an education without due process, the question remains in any given situation just what process is due.[7]

Exactly which procedures may be required to determine a student's guilt or innocence of an offense and to impose punishment depends in large part on the seriousness of the charges and the possible consequences of conviction. At the least, you are entitled to know what you are accused of doing wrong and to have the chance to tell your side of the story. In serious cases, this hearing should take place before an impartial person. You might also have the right to have a lawyer represent you, to call witnesses on your behalf, to question or cross-examine your accusers and the witnesses against you, and to have a transcript made of the proceedings for a possible appeal.

The right to due process also means that any punishment imposed must be in proportion to the offense committed. A serious punishment such as expulsion should not be imposed for a minor infraction of the rules or for the kind of conduct for which other students in the past have received mild punishment.

You should note that the right to due process is only half the battle in obtaining fair treatment in your school. A hearing only guarantees you a chance to show that you did not violate a school rule; it will not determine whether the rule was a fair one in the first place. If, for example, your school has a rule against holding hands in the hall, the right to a hearing won't protect you if you and a friend were in fact holding hands. Therefore, it is important to work for fair rules as well as fair procedures.

How can students know if their school's rules are fair?

If you want to determine whether your school's regulations are reasonable or to convince your school officials to adopt more reasonable policies, there are several guidelines to which you can refer. At the very least, school rules should be directly related to the educational program and have an educational purpose. A Massachusetts Department of Education pamphlet written by students points out the distinction between a reasonable rule and an unreasonable one by explaining that "a rule about being late to school relates to a student's education, but one which prohibits long hair, tasteless clothes or being married or pregnant does not."

Other boards of education have come to similar conclusions which your school might find persuasive. The National School Boards Association's Ad Hoc Committee on Discipline has recommended that school boards clarify disciplinary policies and procedures in the following manner:

Establish a task force composed of parents, teachers, students, administrators, and school board members to survey school safety problems and initiate a specific action plan to be implemented within a specific time.

Involve students, teachers, parents, and administrators in developing and enforcing written disciplinary policies and procedures.

Formally and visibly distribute those written disciplinary policies and procedures.[8]

Similarly, the Michigan State Board of Education recommends that in developing a policy governing school regulations local school districts keep in mind the following principles:

1. The policy must provide notice of what conduct is prohibited or permitted;
2. The rules must be reasonably understandable to the average student;
3. The rules must be rationally related to a valid educational purpose;
4. The rules must be precise so as not to prohibit constitutionally protected activities;
5. The policy must provide students with notice of potential consequences for violating specific rules;
6. The type of punishment specified in the policy must be within the expressed or implied authority of the school district to utilize;
7. The punishment must be of reasonable severity in relation to the seriousness of the misconduct or the number of times the misconduct was committed;
8. A copy of the rules and procedures must be disseminated to all students.[9]

Does a school have to put its rules in writing?

Not necessarily. Many states require local school districts to have written codes of discipline; others do not. A Texas court, for example, upheld student suspensions under a school rule that was not in writing but had been announced at several school assemblies attended by the suspended students.[10] A Massachusetts statute, on the other hand, does not allow a school to enforce a rule unless it has been published, approved by a school committee, filed with the state department of education, and provided free of charge to anyone who requests it.[11] You can find out whether written rules are required in your school by writing to your state education department.

Can students be punished for violating a rule they didn't know existed?

Even if schools need not have written rules, they may not punish you for violating a policy you had no reason to believe existed. If, for example, you sometimes leave school during a free period instead of going to study hall, and students have never been told of a rule or policy forbidding that, it would be illegal to punish you without prior warning. If, however, a teacher specifically tells you not to leave and you do, it is likely that you can be punished even in the absence of a written rule. Indeed, just disobeying a school official is grounds for suspension in most school districts.

How specific do school rules have to be?

Even a written rule can be "void for vagueness" if its wording is so unclear that people of "common intelligence must necessarily guess at its meaning and differ as to its application."[12] Courts have thrown out because of vagueness rules forbidding "conduct inimical to the best interest of the school"[13] and language that "upbraids, abuses or insults any member of the instructional staff,"[14] as well as rules against "willfully loitering in a school building without a lawful purpose"[15] and against possessing "medicine" in school.[16]

Does a school have to tell students what the punishment is for breaking a rule?

Some courts have said that schools must spell out what kinds of discipline may be used for specific infractions. For instance, an Ohio court held that a school could not refuse to include in the yearbook a picture of a student whose hair length violated the school's grooming guidelines because the guidelines had failed to specify the possible punishment for violations.[17] A federal court in Michigan told a school district to revise its proposed student conduct code because it was "extremely vague and general as to possible 'corrective action' to take place in the event of infractions." The court ordered that "the range of corrective action be spelled out for each listed infraction."[18]

In most states, indicating the range of possible disciplinary responses is probably adequate. For instance, in an Illinois case, a student was expelled under a school rule prohibiting drugs that specified suspension and only referred to the possibility of expulsion. The court rejected the student's argument that the rule should have identified exactly which offenses would result in suspension and which in expulsion.[19]

Must a school always follow its own rules?

Yes. Even if a school is not required to have written rules or if it could have specified a more severe punishment for particular misconduct, once it adopts a particular rule it is bound by it. For example, if a school states that one kind of punishment is the maximum disciplinary action for a certain offense, it cannot then impose a more severe punishment. In one case, even though the state law authorized expulsion for violating school rules, the court said that a student could not be expelled for possessing marijuana out of school because, first, the local district failed to follow its own rule requiring other disciplinary alternatives before expulsion and, second, its rule concerning drugs did not specifically apply to off-campus possession.[20]

Are there limits on a school's power to regulate student behavior?

Courts sometimes reject school rules as *ultra vires*; that is, the rules are beyond the authority that is granted to the school by the school board or by state law. In Ohio, for instance, a court held that where a school board specified that a principal should establish rules on clothing and cleanliness, he had no authority to regulate hair length. It reasoned that if the board had wanted hair length regulated, it would have said so.[21] A Kentucky court struck down a school policy of reducing students' grades when they were absent during suspensions because the state law said nothing about academic punishment.[22]

A California court found that school officials, by suspending students for reasons not enumerated in state law and also without first exhausting other legally required means of correction, had frustrated the legislature's goal "to safeguard the constitutional and statutory right of children to a free education by establishing fair procedures which must be followed before that right is withdrawn."[23]

What can a student be suspended for?

The grounds for suspension are usually set out in statute and vary widely from state to state. Arizona, for example, simply allows students to be suspended for "good cause,"[24] while the Louisiana statute describes 17 different grounds for suspension, including making an unfounded accusation against a teacher and violating traffic and safety regulations.[25] Infractions involving weapons, drugs, alcohol, and assault are typically suspendable offenses.

When state law sets out the grounds for suspension, you cannot be suspended by a school district for infractions that are not included, at least implicitly, in those laws. And school districts have the power to put further limits on suspensions. Under New York State law, for instance, a student can be suspended who is "insubordinate or disorderly or whose conduct otherwise endangers the safety, morals, health or welfare of others." But under New York City school regulations, the grounds for suspension are much more limited.[26]

Some states (e.g., Florida and California) require schools to exhaust alternative measures before imposing a suspension, unless the student's behavior is dangerous or seriously disruptive. In some places, suspensions for truancy are specifically forbidden (e.g., Florida and New York City).[27]

If you want to know the precise, legal grounds for suspension in your school (and remember that these are the *only* reasons for which a suspension can be imposed), you should look in your state's education law and the bylaws of your school board. Your principal, the school superintendent, or a school board member can probably tell you where to find these laws.

One final point: Courts have recognized that suspensions are an extreme measure that undermines the basic aim of a school system—namely, to educate its students. When a student is barred from school by suspension, he is of course not being educated. Accordingly, suspensions should be used only as a last resort and only in an emergency, when there is no other alternative. Adhering to this principle, one court stated that a suspension was an administrative device to be used only to remove unruly students at a particularly tense time.[28]

Under this court's reasoning, suspensions should last only as long as the emergency continues. The kind of outbursts of anger that lead to most suspensions usually pass in a matter of minutes or hours. Under such circumstances, there is no reason for a suspension to last more than a day. The regular practice of suspending a student until a hearing several days later is an improper use of the suspension power. School officials have disciplinary powers only for the purpose of furthering education, and suspensions lasting longer than the immediate emergency serve no educational purpose.

The regulations of the New York City Board of Education satisfy these principles.[29] First of all, these regulations call suspension an "emergency" power. Second, they allow suspensions *only* when the student's behavior "prevents the orderly operation of the class or other school activities or presents a clear and present danger of physical injury to school personnel or students." Thus "disobedience" or "abusive language," without disruption or actual danger, is *not* a ground for suspension. Finally, the suspension must be reviewed every day by the principal and may last only as long as the emergency lasts.

Can students be suspended because of their parents' behavior?

No. Punishing a student for the misconduct or inaction of another violates the fundamental right to be free of punishment in the absence of personal guilt.

Some principals and guidance counselors who have tried unsuccessfully to get parents to come to school to discuss their child's work or attitude toward school have suspended the student outright or told the student not to return to school until his or her parents come in. This is illegal. A student can be suspended only for behavior for which the law prescribes suspension. No state makes a parent's failure to come to school grounds for suspending a child.

Nor can other failures of parents to comply with requests of school officials result in a student's suspension. One court, for instance, held that a child's right to attend school did not depend on her mother being present to attend to her medical needs.[30] Likewise, students cannot be suspended or denied access to basic education because of their parents' failure or inability to pay textbook fees.[31]

Finally, even outright misconduct by a parent cannot justify punishing a student. For example, one court has ruled that it was a denial of substantive due process to suspend a student and transfer her to another class because her mother hit her teacher.[32]

What can a student be expelled for?

Generally the power to expel students, *if it exists*, is found in state law. That law will usually say who has the power to expel; in some states (California, for example) only the school board has it. Many states do not permit school officials to expel students at all—that is, to bar them permanently from going to public school in the district. In fact, a permanent expulsion may well be illegal in almost all states in view of the right to an education guaranteed by their constitutions. An Alabama court, however, ruled that a student's suspension for nearly a full school year did not violate the state's compulsory education law.[33]

Some states have laws limiting the expulsion of a student to a certain period of time. In Connecticut, for example, the limit is 180 school days.[34] Generally, too, states restrict expulsion to specific offenses. In Texas, for instance, the only ground for expulsion as the first disciplinary action is assault. (Students found to be "incorrigible" can be transferred to alternative schools. If they continue to be incorrigible, they can be expelled.)[35] In California, a student can be expelled for causing serious physical injury except in self-defense; for possession of a weapon without a lawful use; for unlawful sale of controlled substances other than small quantities of marijuana; and for robbery or extortion.[36]

In any event, the law generally does not permit any government official, such as a school principal, or an agency, such as the school board, to impose any punishment it chooses on a student who breaks a rule. If you disrupt a class and school officials try to expel you, you might bring witnesses to testify at your hearing that other students received only short suspensions for such misconduct. If there is no good reason for giving you a punishment that is so much more severe than that imposed on other students (the fact that you had publicly criticized school policies in an underground newspaper would *not* be a good reason), then the expulsion is illegal.

Can school officials punish students for off-campus activities?

The important question is whether the off-campus misbehavior has any impact on a student's behavior in school. A New
Hampshire court made this distinction when it held that a
student who had come to school drunk could not be punished
by suspension from school until she worked out the psychological problems between herself and her parents. The court
stated that while under certain circumstances suspension might
be appropriate punishment for drunkenness at school, "[i]t is
fundamentally unfair to keep a student out of school indefinitely
because of difficulties between the student and her parents,
unless those difficulties manifest themselves in a real threat to
school discipline."[37] In other words, the school had no business
interfering with a student's problems at home, although it did
have the right to punish a student for misconduct in school
that might be the result of those problems. One federal court
in Texas wrote in a similar vein:

> [I]t makes little sense to extend the influence of school
> administration to off-campus activity under the theory that
> such activity might interfere with the function of educa-
> tion. School officials may not judge a student's behavior
> while he is in his home with his family nor does it seem
> to this court that they should have jurisdiction over his
> acts on a public street corner. . . . Arguably, misconduct
> by students during non-school hours and away from school
> premises could, in certain situations, have such a lasting
> effect on other students that disruption could result during
> the next school day. Perhaps then administrators should
> be able to exercise some degree of influence over off-
> campus conduct. This court considers this power to be
> questionable.[38]

A New Jersey court has held that a student may be temporarily suspended for off-campus acts only if those acts give
school officials "reasonable cause to believe that a student . . .
presents a danger to himself, to others or to school property."[39]
Even that action, the court stated, could be taken only after a
hearing.

Many states and school districts have statutes or rules limiting
authority of schools over out-of-school activities. In California,
Florida, and Louisiana, for instance, schools have jurisdiction
over students' behavior on school grounds, at school-sponsored

activities, and during recesses, as well as on the way to and from school and to and from school activities.[40] Because of these limitations, a federal court of appeals in Louisiana said a student could not be suspended for smoking marijuana off campus.[41] Similarly, the Greensboro, North Carolina, Board of Education restricts its rules against weapons and drugs to "school premises" and "any school activity, function or event."

However, commission of serious criminal acts, including narcotics offenses, has been held to be cause for suspension from school even though the activity took place off campus. A federal court in Texas, for example, upheld a school policy of expelling any student for the rest of the school year for "using, selling, or possessing a dangerous drug" (including marijuana).[42] The court's decision, we believe, represents an unnecessary extension of the responsibility of school officials for off-school activities. Although a principal may be concerned about drug use and wish to warn students about its dangers, it is difficult to accept the position that mere possession of marijuana off campus makes a student a threat to his classmates. Nevertheless, California state law provides for the suspension or expulsion of a student found to have used or sold narcotics or hallucinogens either on or off campus.[43]

In contrast, courts have overruled schools that have punished students for out-of-school activities clearly protected by the First Amendment.[44] For example, a New York student who criticized his high school principal on a radio program went to court when he found that a report of his comments had been placed in his school record. The court ordered the report to be expunged and went on to say, "It is almost inconceivable that in this enlightened day and age a professional administrator could permit the entry in the record of a student of an item which is not only irrelevant but also obviously unconstitutional."[45] In another case a student's right to distribute an underground newspaper off campus was upheld.[46]

If students' off-campus activities result in arrest, can they be suspended even if they have not been convicted?

"One of the most basic concepts of American justice is that [a person] be deemed to be innocent until proven guilty."[47] Since an arrest is only an accusation, punishment prior to a conviction violates that basic concept. Accordingly, the commissioners of education in New York and New Jersey have ruled that suspension on the basis of an arrest alone is illegal.[48]

A school may hold a suspension hearing to try to prove that you actually committed the offense for which you were arrested. If the evidence proves that you committed the offense, and the offense is one related to school activities, you probably can be suspended even before your court trial. In any event, you should consult a lawyer before going to a school hearing that precedes a court appearance since what you say at the first hearing can be used against you at the second. For example, under a Florida statute, a student arrested for a serious crime can be suspended until the case is resolved if the incident "is shown to have an adverse impact on the education program, discipline or welfare in the school in which the student is enrolled."[49] If the student is then convicted of the felony, he or she must be expelled. A Tennessee court ruled that students can be suspended when juvenile court charges are pending against them if it is established at a hearing that "the juvenile poses a danger to persons or property in the school or poses an ongoing threat of disrupting the academic process."[50]

Can students be punished by being forbidden to participate in extracurricular activities without a hearing?

Courts have begun to recognize that extracurricular activities are generally a fundamental part of the school's educational program. To be denied the opportunity to participate in these activities can be as serious a loss of the right to an education as a suspension is. School officials know that prohibiting certain students from playing on a team or going on a class trip would be a more severe punishment than suspending them from school.

A Texas court, for instance, concluded that a student was entitled to *more* due process before being dismissed from an honor society and from a student group organized to foster school spirit, than before being suspended for one day. Membership in both groups required several years of diligent effort. So before the school could forbid the student from participating she was entitled to a hearing.[51]

In an Arkansas case, a federal court ruled that a student could not be suspended from a football team without notice of the charge against him and a chance to present his side of the controversy. The court found that the student had an important interest in participation in interscholastic sports, particularly since he was a senior applying for college athletic scholarships.[52] A New York court held that a student who was charged with drinking a glass of beer in violation of the school's code of conduct for members of athletic teams could not be deprived of his varsity letters without a hearing.[53]

The New York State Commissioner of Education expressed the need for fairness in excluding students from extracurricular activities.[54] In ruling that a school could not prevent students from running for office where it had no evidence that they were responsible for obscene posters, he wrote:

> Full participation in extra-curricular activities may not be restricted on the basis of fiat: to justify such action, there must be a legal basis for curtailment—and, in addition, the extent of disciplinary exclusion must be neither arbitrary, capricious nor unreasonable. . . . Basic fairness dictates that the student and the person in parental relation to him be given an opportunity to appear informally before the administrator authorized to impose discipline and to discuss the factual situation underlying the threatened disciplinary action.[55]

Do students have a right to a hearing every time a teacher or principal wants to punish them?

No, only some of the time. The general rule is that a student has a right to a hearing for serious punishments, but not for minor ones. If a teacher makes a student sit in the back of the room for being noisy, there is no right to a hearing. But if the teacher reports the student to the principal and recommends suspension for the rest of the term, then the student is entitled to a hearing.

Keep in mind that when we speak of a "right to a hearing," we are only speaking of what the law will *require* school officials to do. It may be that the law will require a hearing only when it involves a major disciplinary matter. That does not mean that your school should not be willing, in the interests of fairness, to give you a chance to be heard in any case in which you think you have been treated unjustly. Don't let the fact that you might not have a good court case keep you from insisting on fair treatment at all times.

Do you have a right to due process before you are excluded from transportation to school?

Yes. If you have no other way to get to school, exclusion from the school bus is as serious as suspension or expulsion. However, one court ruled that a hearing on exclusion from the bus could take place *after* bus service to the student was suspended.[56]

May students be excluded from lunch at school for disciplinary reasons?

If students are eligible for free or reduced price meals at school, it is a violation of the National School Lunch Act to discipline them by restricting their access to meals served at school.[57] Even if they do not receive these meals, students should never be prevented from eating lunch *somewhere*. Such a punishment would serve no educational purpose and jeopardize student health and is, therefore, unlawful.

Do you have a right to a hearing before you are transferred to another school for disciplinary reasons?

In many states, yes. In New York, for instance, before a principal even requests a transfer, students are entitled to an informal conference. They are also entitled to have the reasons for the transfer request put in writing. Then students have a right to a formal due process hearing before the superintendent where they may be represented by a lawyer and may present witnesses. A record must be kept of the hearing.[58] In Texas, before students can be transferred to an alternative education program for "incorrigible students," they have a right to a hearing at which it must be shown either that the student presents a clear and present danger of physical harm to self or to others or that the student engages in serious or persistent misbehavior in violation of published standards of student conduct and that "all reasonable alternatives to the pupil's regular classroom program, including a variety of discipline management techniques, have been exhausted."[59]

In numerous cases, courts have ruled that because transfers involve serious consequences for students, they have the right to notice and to due process hearings similar to those required for expulsion.[60] As one court put it: "To transfer a pupil during a school year would be a terrifying experience for many children of normal sensibilities. . . . Realistically, I think many if not most students would consider a short suspension a less drastic form of punishment than an involuntary transfer, especially if the transferee school was farther from home or had poorer physical or educational facilities."[61] In one case where a student was transferred to a GED night school program, a court ordered a formal hearing with an impartial hearing officer who was not an administrator from the student's school. The court observed, "Considering the Board's transfer policy and the fundamental differences between a GED certificate and a standard diploma, this amounts to the functional equivalent of an absolute expulsion."[62]

In addition, find out if the person threatening to transfer you has that power. In many school districts only the superintendent of schools, not the principal, has the power to transfer students.

Who has the power to suspend a student?

In most states only a principal, superintendent, or school board can suspend a student, although some states allow a teacher to suspend, usually for a shorter period of time. If someone other than the principal suspends you, check the state law or school district rules. In most states the suspension is illegal. Sometimes a teacher will just tell you not to come to class but won't call it a suspension. Whatever it's called, not being allowed to go to class has the effect of a suspension and you should request the same rights.

In general, the rule is that the more serious the punishment, the higher the authority required to impose it. For instance, in Ohio either the principal or the superintendent can suspend a student but only the superintendent has the power to expel.[63] In New Jersey, principals and superintendents can impose short term suspensions but only the school board can impose a suspension of over 21 days.[64]

Does a student have the right to a hearing any time he or she is suspended from school?

Yes. In an important decision, *Goss v. Lopez*, reprinted as appendix C to this book, the U.S. Supreme Court held that a "student's legitimate entitlement to a public education [is] a property interest which is protected by the Due Process Clause and . . . may not be taken away for misconduct without adherence to the minimum procedures required by that Clause."[65] The Court went on to state that "the Due Process Clause also forbids arbitrary deprivations of liberty. 'Where a person's good name, reputation, honor or integrity is at stake because of what the government is doing to him,' the minimal requirements of the Clause must be satisfied."

Having recognized that suspending a student from school deprives him of both liberty (his reputation) and property (his education and thus such benefits as a chance for a good job in the future), the Court went on to discuss exactly what procedures must be followed before a student may be suspended from school. The case before the Court involved a 10-day suspension, and thus the opinion dealt only with the minimum due process rights required for short suspensions, suggesting that where longer suspensions are involved, students are entitled to additional due process guarantees. In any case, the Court held that before a student may be suspended for any length of time he must be given oral or written notice of the charges against him and, if he denies them, an explanation of the evidence the authorities have and an opportunity to present his side of the story. The Court further held that, except in emergency situations, the notice of charges and hearing should precede a student's suspension, and where this is not possible because a student poses a danger to persons or property or an ongoing threat of disruption, the notice and hearing "should follow as soon as practicable."

The Supreme Court noted that longer suspensions or expulsions "may require more formal procedures." In fact, many states have passed statutes providing extensive due process protections for both short- and long-term suspensions. Connecticut, for example, has an extensive law providing a system of informal and formal hearings for suspensions of varying lengths and for expulsion, setting time limits on suspensions and expulsion, and providing that suspended students be permitted to complete any classwork and examinations missed during the suspension and that some form of alternative education be arranged for expelled students.[66]

What is the right to adequate notice of charges?
Before you can be severely punished, you have a right to

know the specific acts you are charged with committing. A hearing is useless if you have no idea what accusations you're supposed to be defending yourself against. This idea is one of the oldest in criminal law and is now established in such administrative proceedings as school suspension hearings.

Often a student is charged with "violating school rules" or "serious misconduct"—phrases that fail to give any idea of what offense has been committed or what rule has been violated. That is not adequate notice. A federal court in Washington, D.C., has required that the notice "state specific, clear and full reasons for the proposed action, including the specification of the alleged act upon which the disciplinary action is to be based and the reference to the regulation subsection under which such action is proposed." In addition, some courts have required that, for longer suspensions, the student be provided with a short summary of the evidence to be used against him or her.[67]

A Wisconsin federal court held that a letter given to a student's parents stating "your son . . . continues to conduct himself in an irresponsible and disruptive manner" and "has been deliberately defiant of reasonable requests by teachers . . . on three occasions within the past few weeks" did not satisfy due process requirements of adequate notice of the charges.[68] The court found that the lack of specificity of the charges adversely affected the student's ability to prepare his defense and thus the meaningfulness of his opportunity to be heard.

In addition, courts have held that students have a right to know the charges sufficiently in advance of the hearing to permit them "to examine the charges, prepare a defense and gather evidence and witnesses."[69] The Supreme Court in *Goss* held that the notice given to a student in a case involving the possibility of a short suspension could be either oral or in writing. For longer suspensions, however, other courts have held that notice must be in writing.[70]

In some states, statutes or regulations require schools to provide specific information about charges to students and their parents. The Washington State Administrative Code, for instance, requires advance written notice of charges that includes mention of the proposed punishment and the student's procedural rights.[71] In New York City, before a superintendent can suspend a student, the law requires written notice that includes a list of the school's potential witnesses, the possible consequences of the hearing, the student's due process rights, a list of free or low-cost legal services, and, of course, the specific charges.[72]

A student suspension cannot be based on charges other than those specified to the student in advance of the hearing.[73] In other words, schools cannot charge students with one offense and then find them guilty of another, because to do so would "render meaningless" the "opportunity to present their side of the case," in the words of one judge.[74]

Does a student have the right to an impartial hearing officer at a disciplinary hearing?

For serious punishments you have a right to a hearing before someone who was not involved in the incident and is not prejudiced against you. This will usually be a member of the school board, but sometimes even board members are too involved to be fair judges of your case.

In some states, statutes or regulations specify who may serve as hearing officers. In California, for instance, a hearing panel must consist of three or more school district employees who are not members of the staff of the accused student's school. In Washington, D.C., schools, one court mandated "independent hearing officers" unconnected with the school system for suspensions of over two days.[75] In contrast, the California Supreme Court found nothing wrong with teachers serving as hearing officers.[76]

When hearing officers have had prior involvement in the incidents which led to suspension, a number of courts have overturned the suspensions. For instance, when a Texas student was arrested on a drug charge and the school board discussed the matter with law enforcement officials before suspending him, a federal court ruled that the student was entitled to a hearing before the state commissioner of education.[77]

The New York State Commissioner of Education said that a hearing could not be held before a school superintendent who had been involved at an earlier stage of the case.[78]

A court in Michigan has held that where serious punishment such as transfer was intended, a principal who witnessed the incident leading to the charges could not hear the case.[79]

In another case, a court found an expulsion hearing to be

defective because the school district's attorneys acted as prosecutors and also advised the board that heard the case. Moreover, the superintendent, who was involved in the prosecution, sat in with the board during its deliberations.[80] But in another case, a court refused to find a violation when the school board attorney acted as both prosecutor against the student and advisor to the board.[81] And one court has ruled that a school official is not automatically disqualified from serving on a hearing panel because of prior involvement as an investigator and a witness against the student unless his "involvement in an incident created a bias such as to preclude his affording the student an impartial hearing."[82]

The hearing officer's decision must be made solely on the basis of evidence presented at the hearing, not on privately obtained information. In one case, the New York Commissioner of Education said the decision as to whether the student was guilty could not be based solely on the superintendent's personal knowledge of the student's arrest for alleged drug possession. He wrote:

> It is impossible for the student to cross-examine or in any way rebut the private, nontestimonial knowledge of the hearing officer. . . . [P]erhaps most serious, is the fact that the hearing officer loses his neutral posture and, in effect, becomes a salient witness in support of the charges.[83]

To establish whether the person or board hearing your case may have prejudged it, you should ask for the right to question them about their previous knowledge of the incidents at issue.[84]

Who decides whether the hearing will be open or closed to the public?

The general rule is that a student disciplinary hearing will be closed to the public unless the student, parent, or guardian requests that it be open. The federal law governing privacy of student records can be used to protect the confidentiality of the proceedings.[85] This law prohibits release of student records, either orally or in writing, without written parental consent. (See chapter 11 on student records.) Also, you have the right to exclude from the hearing anyone without a legitimate interest in it. Some courts have also said that you have the right to insist that the hearing be open to the public.[86] However, other courts have ruled that school authorities have the right to keep the public out even against your wishes.[87]

Does a student have the right to be represented by a lawyer at a disciplinary hearing?

Courts have held that students do have this right where serious consequences, such as long-term suspension or expulsion, might result from a hearing.[88] But in *Goss v. Lopez* the Supreme Court explicitly refused to require that students be permitted to be represented by counsel at school disciplinary hearings involving *short* suspensions—ten days or less. The Court made clear, however, that longer suspensions or expulsions might require more formal proceedings, including the right to counsel, and even suggested that in "difficult cases" school officials might permit counsel even though only a short suspension was involved.

Some states, including New York, California, and Texas, specify in statute that students have the right to representation. Some student discipline codes, such as those in Cleveland, Ohio, and Louisville, Kentucky, inform students that they have the right to representation before long-term suspension or expulsion. In California, the student can designate a representative to be present for a hearing on short-term suspension, but the representative cannot act as legal counsel for the student unless the school district also has legal counsel present. In contrast, before an expulsion hearing, the student must receive notice of the right to be represented by counsel.

Another example of consequences serious enough to warrant the right to a lawyer appears in a New York case. There the court ruled that a student had a right to a lawyer when, as a result of being accused of cheating on an examination, she was denied credit for the exam and was prohibited from taking other exams.[89]

No court has ruled that indigent students must be provided with a lawyer free of charge, but some courts have required school districts to provide lists of free or low-cost legal services.[90] If you are threatened with serious punishment and cannot afford a lawyer, you should ask to be given one.

If there are not enough lawyers in your area to represent all the students who need help, you might try to get your parents and other adults to organize a service of nonlawyers trained in the law of student rights to help students in hearings and in other school matters. This has been done effectively in several parts of the country.

Does a student have the right to remain silent at a disciplinary hearing?

The right to remain silent, that is, not to be required to testify against yourself, is guaranteed by the Fifth Amendment to the Constitution. You will rarely have occasion to claim this right, however, as you will almost always want to tell your side of the story. The most likely situation in which you might want to remain silent is when you have had criminal charges brought against you for the same conduct that led to the suspension. If the suspension hearing is held before your criminal trial, you may want to remain silent because what you say about your conduct could be used against you in the criminal trial. Under these circumstances, a federal court has held that "one cannot be denied his Fifth Amendment right to remain silent merely because he is a student."[91] That means your refusal to testify at a disciplinary hearing cannot be used against you as an admission of guilt.

You should probably make such a decision only after consultation with a lawyer. If you and your lawyer think it is important for you to remain silent because of the criminal charges, you might ask that your hearing be postponed until after the criminal trial and that you be allowed to attend classes until the hearing.

Do you have a right to bring witnesses to a disciplinary hearing?

Although the Supreme Court held in *Goss* that students need not be permitted to bring witnesses to a hearing involving suspensions of less than 10 days, courts have held that you have such a right at least for longer suspensions.[92]

The chancellor of the New York City school system held that it was illegal for school officials to deny a student the right to produce a teacher to testify on his behalf by refusing to release the teacher from his duties or pay him for the time he spent at the hearing, since school officials were given time to testify against the student.

If releasing teachers from classroom duties to testify at your hearing is a problem in your case, you might suggest that the hearing be held after school hours.

Do you have the right to question your accusers?

The right to confront and question one's accusers is virtually absolute in criminal law, and the Supreme Court has extended this principle to welfare hearings.[93] The right is equally applicable to school suspensions and other administrative hearings.

School principals sometimes suspend students on the basis of complaints from teachers or other students but refuse to give out the names of these complainants. That the accusers are afraid of retaliation may indeed be a genuine concern. However, the people who wrote the Constitution were even more concerned about the possibility of false charges against innocent persons by anonymous accusers motivated by personal feelings of malice or prejudice.

The problem is illustrated by a New Jersey case involving two girls who had been assaulted by other students. Witnesses to the incident identified the attackers but requested that their names not be revealed because they were afraid of being beaten up themselves. At the hearing, the accused students claimed they were innocent, but they were not permitted to question their accusers. Their case went to the New Jersey Supreme Court, which ruled that the students had a right to question their accusers.[94] The witnesses' fears, the court said, were no basis for denying the accused students their constitutional rights.

Although the U.S. Supreme Court in *Goss* refused to require schools to provide for confrontation of witnesses in connection with *short* suspensions, it again stated that in "unusual circumstances" it might be advisable to allow a student to cross-examine the witnesses against him or her. Most courts in recent years have held that the circumstances of a long-term suspension justify providing the right of cross-examination.[95] In addition, the right is guaranteed by statute in some states.[96]

A Pennsylvania court interpreted the requirement of a "proper hearing" for student suspensions as giving the student an "opportunity to face accusers, hear their testimony, and examine all witnesses testifying against him."[97] A California court said a student could not be suspended for fighting because the facts surrounding the incident were hotly disputed and no witnesses testified at the hearing. Written statements from witnesses were not enough.[98] You should always request the opportunity to confront your accusers. By making them tell the story beyond what is in their written statements or by bringing out inconsistencies in the testimony against you, you may be able to prove your innocence or at least to show there were mitigating factors.

Some courts have ruled that you must be given the names of witnesses whom the school will produce to testify against you,[99] as well as a report on the facts they will testify about.[100] The New Jersey State Commissioner of Education requires that students be given any witnesses' statements before the hearing.[101]

Some school districts go beyond the courts' basic requirements and permit students to question their accusers even at informal short-term suspension conferences. In New York City, for instance, a suspension cannot go on a student's permanent records unless he or she is afforded that right. Whatever the law in your school district, you should always request the opportunity to confront accusers. If you have been falsely accused by someone, questioning that person may be the only way you can establish your innocence.

Do you have to prove you are innocent, or does the school have to prove you are guilty?

Your school or school district bears the burden of proving that you did what they say you did and also that their disciplinary response is appropriate. In the words of one state education commissioner:

Before a pupil may be disciplined, whether it be by expulsion, suspension or curtailment of privileges, two essential elements must be present. There must be some conduct which serves as the predicate for the imposition of discipline and there must be a reasonable degree of certainty that the pupil was the perpetrator of, or otherwise participated in such conduct.

It is clear that the responsibility for establishing both elements in a disciplinary situation rests with the school officials. It is equally well settled that the student must be afforded the basic presumption of innocence of wrongdoing until his guilt has been established by direct, competent evidence of misconduct.[102]

The school can use hearsay evidence such as written statements or testimony by one person about what another person said to him or her concerning the incident. But because of the students' right to question their accusers, a suspension cannot be based on hearsay alone. California law, for instance, states that hearsay alone is inadequate for an expulsion.[103]

The hearing officer must weigh the credibility of the evidence—e.g., is it believable, or inconsistent? Is the witness biased? Does he or she have a motive to lie? The hearing officer cannot automatically give more weight to the school's evidence than to the student's testimony. For instance, one court overturned a suspension where a dean said he had, in principle, accepted a security officer's version of an incident over the student's. The court noted, "[W]hile this 'principle' has wide currency in many totalitarian countries, the court is not aware of its existence as a principle of Anglo-Saxon law."[104]

The burden on the school to prove a student's guilt is not as great as it would be in a criminal court, where guilt has to be proved beyond a reasonable doubt. For example, a school was able to expel a student simply because he had said that cigarettes in his possession contained marijuana, according to a Michigan court.[105] A series of Florida cases involving the sale of caffeine pills illustrates the different sorts of evidence required to prove wrongdoing. The court said the school could expel students who said they had been buying or selling "speed," the street name for amphetamines, a controlled substance, even though the pills were actually caffeine and were neither controlled nor illegal. The students' statements to school officials showed they thought they were dealing in drugs; thus, their statements were adequate grounds for expulsion. But the court argued that a third student could not be expelled, even though she too had been selling caffeine pills, because there was no evidence she had represented them to be "speed."[106]

Courts are reluctant to second guess school districts when it comes to student discipline. Generally, they will overturn a suspension if there is clearly no evidence offered of wrongdoing or if the school district's action violates the student's constitutional rights or is arbitrary or capricious. They might rehear all the evidence and draw their own conclusion if the school district has not kept a record of the original hearing.[107] But they are unlikely to overturn a suspension or expulsion simply because it is excessive punishment even when they come right out and say that it is. This happened in a Mississippi case where the students were expelled for a single act of graffiti (painting the number "1" on a school wall). The court disapproved of the punishment and urged the school system not to impose it, but said, "[D]issatisfactions with such rules must be addressed to the school board, not the courts of this state."[108]

Does the school have to make a record of a disciplinary hearing?

It would be difficult if not impossible to challenge the outcome of a disciplinary hearing without a complete record of what went on at the hearing. For this reason, a number of courts have required schools to maintain a verbatim record and make it available to the student on request.[109] Generally, a tape recording is all that is required, but some courts have said that schools must make a complete written transcript of the tape and provide it to the student if he or she so requests.[110] Other courts have said a student has a right to make a recording of the hearing.[111] Some states, including New York, Ohio, and Washington, require schools to maintain verbatim records. But note that, as a general rule, this requirement only pertains to longer suspensions or expulsions.

Is a student entitled to written findings after a hearing?

To appeal a suspension, it is important to have a written decision that discusses the testimony and states the reason for imposing the suspension; otherwise, the person reviewing the case on appeal cannot determine whether there was a legal basis for the suspension.

Most courts that have dealt with this issue have agreed that students are entitled to a written statement of the factual findings behind the hearing officer's decision.[112] Written findings may also be required by your state's statutes or regulations. Washington State, for instance, provides that students receive "written findings of fact and conclusions."[113]

As the result of a case in New York City, hearing officers must notify students of their decision by telephone or mailgram within two days of the hearing and must mail out a written decision within five days. This written decision must explain the reasons for the determination, indicate the relevant evidence, and include factual findings as well as specify where and when the student can return to school. The decision must be implemented within five days of the hearing.[114]

Does the student have a right to appeal an adverse decision?
Most school districts permit an appeal after the suspension or expulsion hearing, and many states spell out appeal procedures in their statutes concerning student discipline. Typically, an appeal goes to the superintendent and then to the school board. In some states, students have the right to a further appeal to the state commissioner or state board of education. The letter advising you of your suspension should provide information on how to appeal. If it does not, you should ask your school board office or state department of education. You can appeal based on the school's failure to follow proper procedures, the lack of evidence, the excessiveness of the punishment, the unfairness of the rule, or anything else that is unfair or in violation of established policy. You should refer to the record of the hearing and to the hearing officer's written findings if they exist. (If no record or findings exist, that in itself is a ground for appeal.) You can ask to be returned to school, to be moved to another school, to have the suspension removed from your record, etc.

Although some courts have guaranteed the right to appeal,[115] appeals after hearings are not always required.[116] If your school district or state has no appeal procedures, you may have to go to court to challenge your suspension.

Is a student entitled to instructional services during a long-term suspension?
Some states, including New York, New Jersey, and Connecticut, require schools to provide alternative instruction to students of compulsory-attendance age. The New York State Commissioner of Education has ruled that this instruction must be adequate to enable the student to complete all of his or her coursework. If, for instance, the student was taking typing, a typewriter must be available. If the student was enrolled in a Spanish class, a Spanish tutor must be provided.[117] The New Jersey State Commissioner of Education ruled that a suspended student must have the opportunity to make up work missed.[118] In one New York case, a judge said that even though the student

was suspended for only five days, giving him homework assignments was not enough. The school should have also provided tutoring because of applicable state law.[119]

In some school districts, students may be transferred to an alternative education site *instead* of being expelled. These in-school suspensions are increasingly used as an alternative to short-term suspensions. But as the Kentucky Department of Education notes in its *Student Discipline Guidelines*, this is "a common practice among schools seeking to avoid the complications of actual suspension" and is unacceptable unless the student is placed in a program that provides close supervision and structured study. A Kentucky Attorney General's Opinion concludes, " 'In-school suspension' is a contradiction in terms and not within the disciplinary procedures authorized by statute, and if an 'in-school suspended' child is not being afforded an alternative educational program and school counseling, the child is legally absent from school."[120] Whether or not they offer alternative instruction, in-school suspensions remove students from their regular classrooms and should therefore entitle them to the same due process protections as out-of-school suspensions of the same duration.

Can a student who is above the age of compulsory school attendance be discharged from school without due process?

The right to go to school lasts longer than the obligation. While you may not be *compelled* to attend school past the age of 16 or 17, you usually have a *right* to attend until you are 21 (check your state's law for the exact ages). Students above the compulsory attendance age have all of the same due process rights as younger students.

What should you do if you believe your school's disciplinary procedures are followed in a racially discriminatory manner?

Federal Office of Civil Rights statistics reveal that minority students are suspended at dramatically higher rates than are white students.[121] In a landmark case in 1974, a federal court found that racial disparities in disciplinary action in Dallas came from illegal discrimination and did not simply reflect more misbehavior by minority students. The court said several factors contributed to the disparity, including: (1) the tendency of school staff to refer minority students for discipline more frequently and punish them more harshly than whites for equivalent conduct; (2) punishment for cultural differences such as wearing hats or different styles of personal conduct; and (3) provocation of minority students as a result of "insensitivity," "personal racism," "institutional racism," and the very existence of a "white-controlled institution."[122] In a similar challenge in Newburgh, New York, a school district agreed to a timetable of eliminating racial disparity in its suspension rates. The district consented to set up committees composed of teachers, students, parents, community representatives, and the principal from each school. These committees would consider proposals to change and clarify the discipline code, to provide assistance to teachers with high discipline referral rates, to tutor students whose behavior problems were related to low achievement, etc. The school district also said it would increase the percentage of minority teachers and train all school staff in race relations and discipline.[123]

In a third case, in Arkansas, a court found that school rules were vague and allowed for too much discretion by teachers. This resulted in black students being disciplined for certain behavior for which white students were not. The court ordered that "uniform and objective guidelines be established to eliminate the opportunity to administer discipline on an uneven handed basis."[124] Courts have considered disciplinary practices in the course of designing remedies for unconstitutional segregation of schools. For instance, in a Benton Harbor, Michigan, desegregation case, the court ordered that a biracial committee develop a uniform discipline code to include an appeal procedure to a biracial panel in the case of suspension or expulsion. The court also stated that the "use of suspension or expulsion should be limited to a last resort and the committee should explore the use of effective alternatives to suspension or expulsion."[125]

If you believe that your school is guilty of racially discriminatory practices or of excessive use of suspensions and expulsions, you should seek the help of local civil rights or student advocacy groups to convince the school to adopt more evenhanded and educationally sound practices. You can obtain recent suspension data on your school district from the National Coalition of Advocates for Students in Boston. You can also file a freedom of information request with your school district, which should collect data on the rate of suspensions for specific offenses among various ethnic and racial groups. In New York City, this data revealed that minority students were suspended more frequently than other students for smoking, truancy, lateness, and poor academic achievement. The Board of Education eventually signed an agreement with the Office of Civil Rights not to suspend anyone for these offenses.

NOTES

1. National School Boards Association, *Towards Better and Safer Schools* (1984), p. 18.
2. G. P. Sorenson, "The Worst Kinds of Discipline," *Update on Law-Related Discipline* (Fall 1982), p. 27.
3. *Towards Better and Safer Schools*, p. 18.
4. *Id.*, p. 9.
5. Dr. Gary Gottfredson, Oversight Hearings on School Discipline, House Subcommittee on Elementary, Secondary, and Vocational Education, 1/23/84.
6. *Goss v. Lopez*, 419 U.S. 565 (1975).
7. *Morrissey v. Brewer*, 408 U.S. 471, 481 (1972).
8. *Towards Better and Safer Schools*, p. 231.
9. Michigan State Board of Education, *A Recommended Guide to Students' Rights and Responsibilities in Michigan, Second Edition* (May 1982), p. 41.
10. *New Braunfels Independent School Dist. v. Armke*, 658 S.W.2d 330 (Tex. 10th Dist. 1983).
11. Mass. Gen. Laws chap. 71, §37H.
12. *Hynes v. Mayor and Council of Borough of Oradell*, 425 U.S. 610, 620 (1976).
13. *Mitchell v. King*, 363 A.2d 68 (Conn. 1976).
14. *McCall v. State*, 354 So.2d 869 (Fla. 1978).
15. *State v. Martinez*, 538 P.2d 521 (Wash. 1975).
16. *Bertens v. Stewart*, 453 So.2d 92 (Fla. App. 2d Dist. 1984).
17. *McClung v. Board of Education*, 346 N.E.2d 691 (Ohio 1976).
18. *Bradley v. Milliken*, 540 F.2d 229, (E.D. Mich. 1975).
19. *M. v. Board of Education*, 429 F. Supp. 288 (S.D. Ill. 1977).
20. *Galveston Independent School Dist. v. Boothe*, 590 S.W.2d 553 (Tex. Civ. App. 1979).
21. *Cordova v. Chanko*, 315 F. Supp. 953 (N.D. Ohio 1970).

22. *Dorsey v. Bale*, 521 S.W.2d 76 (Ky. App. Ct. 1975).

23. *Slayton v. Pomona Unified School Dist.*, 207 Calif. Rptr. 705 (2d Dist. 1984).

24. Ariz. §15-843.

25. Louisiana §17:416.

26. N.Y. Educ. Law §3214(3)(a)(1).

27. Fla. Stat. §236.26(1)(b); Calif. Educ. Code. §48900; New York City Chancellor's Regulation A-441, "Suspension of High School Students," 7/1/83.

28. *Williams v. Dade County School Board*, 441 F.2d 299 (5th Cir. 1971).

29. Chancellor's Regulation A-441, "Suspension of High School Students," 7/1/83.

30. *Hairston v. Drosick*, 423 F. Supp. 180 (S.D. W.Va. 1976).

31. *Carder v. Mich. City School Corp.*, 552 F. Supp. 869 (N.D. Ind. 1982).

32. *St. Ann v. Palisi*, 495 F.2d 423 (5th Cir. 1974).

33. *Adams v. City of Dothan Board of Education*, 485 So.2d 757 (Ala. Civ. App. 1986).

34. Conn. Gen. Stat. §10-233a(e).

35. Tex. Public Schools Code Ann. §21.3011.

36. Calif. Educ. Code §48915.

37. *Cook v. Edwards*, 341 F. Supp. 307 (D.N.H. 1972).

38. *Sullivan v. Houston Independent School District*, 307 F. Supp. 1328 (S.D. Tex. 1969), cert. denied, 414 U.S. 1032 (1973).

39. *R.R. v. Board of Education*, 109 N.J. Super. 337, 263 A.2d 180 (1970).

40. Calif. Educ. Code §48900(1); Fla. Stat. §232.25; La. Rev. Stat. Ann. §416.

41. *Abadie v. St. Bernard Parish School Board*, 485 So.2d 596 (La. App. 4th Cir. 1986).

42. *Caldwell v. Cannady*, 340 F. Supp. 835 (N.D. Tex. 1972).

43. Calif. Educ. Code §48915.

44. See chapter 2, "First Amendment Rights."

45. *Matter of Shakin v. Schuker*, Index No. 6312/71 (Sup. Ct. Queens Co. 11/16/71).

46. *Sullivan v. Houston Independent School District, supra.*

47. *Matter of Rodriguez*, 8 Ed. Dept. Rep. 214 (1969).

48. *Matter of Rodriguez, supra; Diggs v. Board of Education of Camden*, 1970 Schl. L. Dec. 225. See also *Howard v. Clark*, 299 N.Y.S.2d 65 (Sup. Ct. 1969), in which the court found that arrest was not one of the grounds set out for suspension in state law.

49. Fla. Stat. §232.26.

50. *Brown v. Board of Education of Tipton County*, Civil Action No. 79-2234-M (W.D. Tenn. 5/3/79).

51. *Ector County Independent School Dist. v. Hopkins*, 518 S.W.2d 576 (Tex. Civ. App. 1974).

52. *Boyd v. Board of Directors of the McGehee School Dist. No. 17*, 612 F. Supp. 86 (E.D. Ark. 1985).

53. *O'Connor v. Board of Education of School Dist. No. 1*, 316 N.Y.S.2d 799 (Sup. Ct. 1970).

54. *Matter of Stewart*, 21 Ed. Dept. Rep. 654 (1982).

55. *Matter of Port*, 9 Ed. Dept. Rep. 107 (1970).

56. *Rose v. Nashua Board of Education*, 679 F.2d 279 (1982).

57. 42 U.S.C. §1751 *et seq.*

58. N.Y. Educ. Law §3214(5).

59. Tex. Public Schools Code Ann. §21.301.

60. *Betts v. Board of Education, supra; Mills v. Board of Education, supra; Jordan v. School Dist. of City of Erie, Pa.*, 583 F.2d 91 (3d Cir. 1978).

61. *Everett v. Marcase*, 426 F. Supp. 397, 400 (E.D. Pa. 1977).

62. *Quintanilla v. Carey*, Civil Action No. 75-C-829 (N.D. Ill. 3/31/75).

63. Ohio Rev. Code Ann. §3313.66.

64. N.J.S.A. §18A:37-4, 37-5.

65. *Goss v. Lopez*, 419 U.S. 565 (1975).

66. Conn. Gen. Stat. §§10-233(a) *et seq.*

67. *Mills v. Board of Education of the District of Columbia*, 348 F. Supp. 866 (D. D.C. 1972); *Vail v. Board of Education of Portsmouth School Dist.*, 354 F. Supp. 592 (D.N.H. 1973); *Quintanilla v. Carey*, Civil Action No. 75-C-829 (N.D. Ill., 3/31/75).

68. *Keller v. Fochs*, 385 F. Supp. 262 (E.D. Wis. 1974).

69. *Sullivan v. Houston Independent School District*, 307 F. Supp. 1328 (S.D. Tex. 1969); *Fielder v. Board of Education of School District of Winnebago (Nebraska)*, 346 F. Supp. 722 (D. Nebr. 1972); *Caldwell v. Cannady*, 340 F. Supp. 835 (N.D. Tex. 1972); *Esteban v. Central Missouri State College*, 277 F. Supp. 649 (W.D. Mo. 1967), *aff'd*, 415 F.2d 1077 (8th Cir. 1969), *cert. denied*, 398 U.S. 965 (1970).

70. *Pervis v. LaMarque Independent School District*, 466 F.2d 1054 (5th Cir. 1972).

71. Wash. Ad. Code. §180-40-140.

72. *Boe v. Board of Education*, 80 Civ. 2829 (S.D.N.Y. 1/22/85).

73. *Strickland v. Inlow*, 519 F.2d 744, 747 (8th Cir. 1975).

74. *John A. v. San Bernardino City Unified School Dist.*, 654 P.2d 242 (Calif. 1982).

75. *Mills v. Board of Education*, 348 F. Supp. 866 (D.D.C. 1972).

76. *John A. v. San Bernardino, supra.*

77. *Caldwell v. Cannady*, 340 F. Supp. 835 (N.D. Tex. 1972). See also *French v. Bashful*, 303 F. Supp. 1333 (E.D. La. 1969), *appeal dismissed*, 425 F.2d 182 (5th Cir. 1970).

78. *Matter of Dishaw*, 10 Ed. Dept. Rep. 34 (1970). See also *Gratton v. Winooski School District*, Civil Action No. 74-86 (D. Vt. 4/10/74); *Jordan v. School District of Erie*, Civil Action No. 34-75 (W.D. Pa. 2/5/74).

79. *Detroit Board of Education v. Scott*, Civil Action No. 176-814 (Cir. Ct. Mich. 1/12/72). See also *Murray v. West Baton Rouge Parish School Board*, 472 F.2d 438 (5th Cir. 1973); *Quintanilla v. Carey*, Civil Action No. 75-C-829 (N.D. Ill. 3/31/75).

80. *Gonzales v. McEuen*, 435 F. Supp. 460 (C.D. Calif. 1977).

81. *Tasby v. Estes*, 643 F.2d 1103 (5th Cir. 1981).

82. *Brewer v. Austin Independent School Dist.*, 779 F.2d 260 (5th Cir. 1985).

83. *Matter of DeVore*, 11 Ed. Dept. Rep. 296 (1972).

84. *Hobson v. Bailey*, 309 F. Supp. 1393 (W.D. Tenn. 1970).

85. 20 U.S.C. §1232.

86. *Moore v. Student Affairs Committee*, 284 F. Supp. 725 (M.D. Ala. 1968); *Mills, supra.*

87. *Linwood v. Board of Education*, 463 F.2d 763 (7th Cir.), *cert. denied*, 409 U.S. 1027 (1972).

88. *Givens v. Poe*, 346 F. Supp. 202 (W.D. N.C. 1972); *Goldwyn v. Allen*, 281 N.Y.S.2d 899 (Sup. Ct. 1967); *Quintanilla v. Carey*, Civil Action No. 75-C-829 (N.D. Ill. 3/31/75). See also *Gratton v. Winooski School District*, Civil Action No. 74-86 (D. Vt. 4/10/74); *Jordan v. School District of Erie*, Civil Action No. 34-75 (W.D. Pa. 2/5/74).

89. *Goldwyn v. Allen*, 281 N.Y.S.2d 899 (Sup. Ct. 1967).

90. *Mills v. Board of Education of the District of Columbia, supra; Jordan v. School District of Erie, Supra.*

91. *Caldwell v. Cannady*, 340 F. Supp. 835 (N.D. Tex. 1972).

92. *Givens v. Poe*, 346 F. Supp. 202 (W.D. N.C. 1972); *Quintanilla v. Carey*, Civil Action No. 75-C-829 (N.D. Ill. 3/31/75).

93. *Goldberg v. Kelly*, 397 U.S. 254 (1970).

94. *Tibbs v. Board of Education of the Township of Franklin*, 114 N.J. Super. 287, 276 A.2d 165 (1971), *aff'd*, 284 A.2d 179 (N.J. 1971).

95. *Fielder v. Board of Education of School District of Winnebago (Nebraska)*, 346 F. Supp. 722 (D. Neb. 1972); *De Jesus v. Penberthy*, 344 F. Supp. 70 (D. Conn. 1972); *Givens v. Poe*, 346 F. Supp. 202 (W.D.N.C. 1972); *Quintanilla v. Carey*, Civil Action No. 75-C-829

(N.D. Ill. 3/31/75). See also *Gratton v. Winooski School District*, Civil Action No. 74-86 (D. Vt. 4/10/74); *Jordan v. School District of Erie*, Civil Action No. 34-75 (W.D. Pa. 2/5/74).

96. See, e.g., N.Y. State Educ. Law §3214(3); Conn. Public Act No. 75-609 (7/8/75), An Act Concerning Exclusion from School for Disciplinary Purposes.

97. *Scott v. Trinity Area School Dist.*, 53 D & C 2d 488 (Pa. 1971).

98. *John A. v. San Bernardino, supra.*

99. *Hobson v. Bailey*, 309 F. Supp. 1393 (W.D. Tenn. 1970).

100. *Caldwell v. Cannady*, 340 F. Supp. 835 (N.D. Tex. 1972).

101. *Scher v. Board of Education of West Orange*, 1969 Sch. L. Dec. 92.

102. *Matter of DeVore, supra.*

103. Calif. Educ. Code §48918(f).

104. *Giles v. Redfern*, Clearinghouse No. 20, 624 (N.H. Sup. Ct. Cheshire Cty. 1/18/77).

105. *Birdsey v. Grand Blanc Community Schools*, 344 N.W. 2d 342 (1983).

106. *McEntire v. Brevard Cty. School Board*, 471 So.2d 1287 (Fla. Ct. App. 1985).

107. *Tomlinson by Tomlinson v. Pleasant Valley School Dist.*, 479 A.2d 1169 (Pa. 1984).

108. *Clinton Municipal Separate School Dist. v. Byrd*, 477 So.2d 237 (Miss. Sup. Ct. 1985).

109. *Mills, supra, Jordan, supra.*

110. *Ross v. Disare*, 500 F. Supp. 928 (S.D. N.Y. 1977); *Boe v. Board of Education, supra.*

111. *Marzette v. McPhee*, 294 F. Supp. 562 (W.D. Wis. 1968); *Givens v. Poe, supra*; *Quintanilla v. Carey, supra.*

112. *De Jesus v. Penberthy*, 344 F. Supp. 70 (D. Conn. 1976); *Boe v. Board of Education, supra*; *Jordan, supra*; *Mills, supra. Contra: Linwood v. Board of Education, supra.*

113. Wash. Ad. Code §180-40-140(1).

114. *Boe v. Board of Education, supra.*

115. *Berry v. School Dist. of the City of Benton Harbor*, 515 F. Supp. 344 (W.D. Mich. 1981); *Bradley v. Milliken, supra*; *Mills, supra.*

116. *Brewer v. Austin, supra.*

117. *Matter of Gesner*, 20 Ed. Dept. Rep. 326 (1980).

118. *Haddad v. Cranford Board of Education*, 1968 S.L.D. 98.

119. *Turner v. Kowalski*, 374 N.Y.S.2d 133 (A.D. 2d Dept. 1975).

120. Ky. OAG 77-419.

121. Office of Civil Rights, U.S. Dept. of Education, "1984 Elementary and Secondary School Civil Rights Survey, Dist. Summary," June 1986, prepared by DBS Corp.

122. *Hawkins v. Coleman,* 376 F. Supp. 1330 (N.D. Tex. 1974).
123. *Ross v. Saltmarsh,* Civil Action No. 38723 (W.D.N.Y. 5/14/80).
124. *Sherpell v. Humnoke School Dist. No. 5,* 619 F. Supp. 670 (E.D. Ark. 1985) appeal dismissed, 814 F.2d 538.
125. *Berry v. School Dist. of the City of Benton Harbor,* 515 F. Supp. 344 (W.D. Mich. 1981).

V

Law Enforcement and Searches

Fear of drugs and violence has led many schools to increase the practice of searching students and even to conduct mass searches. Certain cities have deployed undercover police in the schools, sometimes masquerading as students, to catch drug dealers. These days security guards and uniformed police are seen more frequently in schools.

What is an appropriate balance between the need to keep drugs and weapons out of schools and your *right* to privacy? Schools are more likely to be safe and orderly when students are made to feel welcome—to feel they really belong. Police-state tactics not only violate your rights, they also are not the most effective way to address school discipline and safety problems.

When school officials infringe so blatantly on a student's privacy, they unintentionally teach disrespect for the rights and needs of others and destroy an atmosphere conducive to learning. Once a school reaches the point where students are being watched by surveillance devices, fingerprinted for identification, eavesdropped on in class by undercover police agents, or confronted in the halls by security guards, education becomes difficult if not impossible.

May school officials allow police into schools to question or arrest students?

Yes, but neither school officials nor anybody else can make students talk to the police. You have a constitutional right to remain silent. The practice in some schools, however, is for school officials to cooperate with police investigations by taking students from class and making them available for questioning. Other states and local school districts have set limits on this practice. In New York City, for instance, schools may only allow police to conduct investigations in school if the alleged offense was committed on school property. School officials cannot require students to submit to an interview with the police in school, and a school official must stay with a student who agrees to be questioned. The principal cannot allow police to remove a student from school unless the student is under arrest. If the student is arrested, the parent or guardian must be notified and a school official must stay with the student until the parent arrives.[1]

The Cleveland, Ohio, schools provide detailed instructions for principals regarding student interrogation by police:[2]

When law enforcement authorities want to question a student at school, the principal must try to contact the student's parent or guardian to give the authorities permission to do so. The parent or guardian may refuse; request interrogation only in his/her presence; or request that the principal act in the role of the parent during the interrogation.

If the parent or guardian cannot be reached, the principal may deny or allow the questioning.

Whenever the principal acts in the place of the parent or legal guardian, the principal must:

a. Assure that the student has been advised of his/her rights
b. Be present during the entire interrogation
c. Not enter into the interrogation on behalf of the authority
d. Interrupt the interrogation to protect the pupil from abusive or threatening questioning
e. End the interrogation when it becomes obvious that a formal charge is likely

Many school district policies and discipline codes *require* school officials to call in police whenever a crime, including possession of a weapon or drugs, is committed on school grounds.

What should students do to protect themselves in interviews with the police?

You have the right to remain silent, and this is usually the best course to take. You should give the police your name and address. If they don't know who you are, they may be more likely to arrest you since they won't be able to get in touch with you any other way. Until you have spoken to your parents or a lawyer, don't answer any questions—even if the school authorities say it is in your best interest to do so, or even if the police have said you will not be allowed to leave until you have answered their questions.

There are occasions when nothing bad would come of answering a few questions on the spot to clear up a simple misunderstanding; you must use your own judgment. You should keep in mind, however, that it is the job of the police to investigate crimes. If you have any reason to believe that you are suspected of committing a crime, don't explain, don't lie, don't confess. Don't talk, except to ask to call your parents or a lawyer. It's far better to err on the side of caution and not answer questions. This includes questioning by school officials, since what you say to a school official can be used against you in a criminal prosecution or in a suspension/expulsion hearing. For example, a California court upheld the conviction of a student on the basis of testimony by his high school principal that the student had confessed in response to the principal's questioning to having purchased marijuana in school.[3] The court held that the principal, not being a police officer, was not required to warn the student of his right to remain silent before questioning him, and thus the confession was admissible evidence.[4]

Can a school official search a student?

Generally speaking, yes. In *New Jersey v. T.L.O.*, the Supreme Court ruled that students in school enjoy Fourth Amendment protections against unreasonable searches of their persons and property. The Court found that school authorities act as public officials, not private citizens, when they search students and such searches are, therefore, limited by the Fourth Amendment. A majority of the justices, however, refused to apply to searches of students the usual Fourth Amendment requirements that before searching a citizen a government official must have a warrant signed by a judge or the express consent of the person searched. The Court said that requiring a warrant based on probable cause for student searches would "unduly interfere with the maintenance of the swift and informal disciplinary procedures needed in schools."[5] It therefore ruled that school officials can search a student:

> when there are reasonable grounds for suspecting that the search will turn up evidence that the student has violated

or is violating either the law or the rules of the school. Such a search will be permissible in its scope when the measures adopted are reasonably related to the objectives of the search and not excessively intrusive in light of the age and sex of the student and the nature of the infraction.[6]

This means that to be reasonable under *T.L.O.*, a school search must pass two tests. First, the school official must have good reason to think evidence of wrongdoing will be found. Second, the search must not be more intrusive than necessary to find the specific thing the school official expects to find.

The Supreme Court decision sets out the student's *minimum* rights against unreasonable school searches. But states are free to set *stricter* standards than "reasonable suspicion" under their state laws and constitution, and school districts can further restrict them. Louisiana, for instance, requires full probable cause for personal searches of students through its statutes and case law.[7] For the most part, however, state courts have adopted the *T.L.O.* "reasonable suspicion" or "reasonable grounds" standards for school searches. These courts have listed a number of factors to be considered in determining whether there is sufficient cause to search a student. These include the student's age, history, and school record, as well as the prevalence and seriousness of the problem and the presence of exigent circumstances requiring a search without delay or further investigation. Schools should also consider the probative value and reliability of the information used to justify the search and the particular school official's prior experience with the student.[8]

In several cases state courts have found that school officials lacked sufficient cause for a student search. The California Supreme Court found unlawful a school principal's search of a student whom he suspected of being tardy or truant and who was carrying a bag with an "odd looking bulge." When the principal attempted to see the bag, the student held it behind his back and told him he needed a warrant. The court found that these facts did not add up to a "reasonable suspicion" that the student was engaged in unlawful activity.[9]

Similarly, the highest court in New York found no reasonable grounds for a drug search after a student had been seen twice within one hour entering a restroom with a fellow student and leaving within 5 to 10 seconds. According to the court these trips "could be explained by all sorts of innocent activities." In general, the court emphasized that "although the necessities for a public school search may be greater than for one outside the school, the psychological damage that would be risked on sensitive children by random search insufficiently justified by the necessities is not tolerable."[10]

In Florida, a court found that an assistant principal did not have reasonable suspicion sufficient to justify searching a student when his female friend fainted at school, reportedly because she had taken drugs.[11]

Can students be subjected to mass searches?

No. The Supreme Court did not have to deal with this question in the *T.L.O.* case because the teacher's accusation pointed to only one student. But a number of federal and state courts have ruled that there must be reasonable suspicion directed specifically at each student before a school official can search students. For instance, in two Texas cases, federal courts ruled that a sniff search around students' bodies by police dogs trained to detect drugs was unconstitutional because there was no individualized suspicion.[12] Similarly, a state court in Washington ruled that school officials did not have reasonable suspicion when they made students agree to a search of their luggage as a condition for participating in a band concert without a particularized suspicion that contraband would be found with respect to each student searched.[13] In the same vein, a federal court in New York ruled that it was unreasonable to strip-search an entire fifth-grade class in order to identify the student who had stolen three dollars.[14] Similarly, routine searches of every student referred to a dean for breaking a school rule or random searches on Halloween to deter pranks violate the rule that individualized reasonable suspicion is required as a basis for a student search.

Can schools perform strip searches on students?

Although courts have not banned strip searches outright, two important rules limit their use. First, the Supreme Court in *T.L.O.* prohibited searches that are "excessively intrusive." If a teacher were looking for a gun or large knife, a pat-down would be enough to determine whether the student had the weapon. A search for a small bag of missing candy might require a more intrusive search, but one that could not be justified in light of the relative unimportance of the infraction.

Second, a number of courts have ruled that the more intrusive the search, the higher the degree of suspicion required. A federal court in New York, for instance, found that the teacher had reasonable suspicion to search a student's handbag for stolen money but should not have strip-searched the student without full probable cause.[15] Along the same lines, a federal court in Indiana ruled that a strip search of students based on a sniffer dog's alert was illegal: "[T]he conduct of the school officials in permitting such a nude search was not only unlawful but outrageous under settled indisputable principles of law."[16] A federal court in Ohio ruled that although there was enough particularized suspicion that specific students had marijuana to warrant asking them to empty their pockets, the school official's authority to conduct reasonable searches could not justify a degrading search of a student's body cavities.[17]

In some communities, outrage over particular search incidents has resulted in school boards passing detailed search policies to protect student rights. In Louisville, Kentucky, for instance, such detailed search procedures were promulgated following an episode where an entire third grade class was strip-searched because four dollars collected in a raffle was missing. The new rules require reasonable individualized suspicion and limit searches to accessories and outer garments. In cases where school officials believe that students possess evidence that could result in criminal charges or that a search may require "disrobing to the skin," the search must be conducted by law enforcement officers.[18]

After a similar incident involving children, the Columbia, South Carolina, school district adopted a full probable cause standard for strip searches of students. There, searches must be authorized and supervised by the principal, and students cannot be asked to expose underwear or private parts of the body.[19]

Can school officials search students' lockers and desks?

One thing should be said here before anything else: Do not put anything in your locker or desk that you would not want the police or school officials to see.

State courts, statutes, and local practices vary widely on the question of when students' lockers and desks can be searched. But one thing is certain: School officials have fewer restrictions on searching lockers and desks than on searching persons, and in many places they are much freer.

In one New York case a vice-principal conducted a search at the direction of a police officer who suspected the student possessed drugs; the court upheld the search on the ground that the student had no reasonable expectation of privacy since he knew the principal had a master key to all the locks.[20] Other courts have said schools can conduct locker searches triggered by drug-detecting dogs, because the school exercises control over the lockers.[21]

In contrast, the California Supreme Court makes no distinction between personal searches and searches of lockers; in both situations it requires reasonable and individualized suspicion.[22] Like California, New Jersey insists there be definite grounds for suspicion in order to search a locker. The New Jersey Supreme Court ruled that it was unlawful to search a locker in a case where a police officer had received an anonymous call from someone claiming to be the parent of another student and naming a certain student as a drug dealer. The officer passed this information on to the school and an assistant principal searched the student's locker. The court found the information did not amount to reasonable suspicion and ruled that reasonable suspicion was required for a locker search if, as in this case, the student was justified in believing that the master key to the locker would be employed only at his request or convenience.[23] If the school had a publicized policy of regularly inspecting student lockers, the suspected student might not have had the same expectation of privacy.

A number of states have statutes insisting upon reasonable suspicion before lockers can be searched but do not require search warrants. Louisiana law, for instance, states that any teacher, principal, or administrator can search any "building, desk, locker, area or grounds" for contraband "when he has articulable facts which lead him to a reasonable belief that the items sought will be found."[24]

Similarly, both Florida and Maryland permit searches of student lockers if there is reasonable suspicion that a prohibited object is contained in the area to be searched. Both states require schools to notify students that these places are subject to search. Maryland limits such searches to items illegal under state law and requires that a third party be present when a locker is searched.[25]

Many local school districts have written policies on locker searches which may or may not protect your privacy. The Detroit Board of Education Policy on Discipline and Student Rights permits locker searches but states "there must be reason to believe that the student is using his/her locker, desk or other property in such a way as to endanger his/her own health or safety or the health, safety and rights of other persons." In contrast, the Jackson, Mississippi, policy states that "desks and lockers are public property and school authorities may conduct an inspection for any reason related to school administration." Whether or not you have a reasonable expectation of privacy in your locker or desk may depend on the stated policy of your particular school.

Can schools require students to submit to blood and urine tests for drugs?

No. As more school districts impose such tests in an attempt to combat drug and alcohol use, there is bound to be litigation challenging their legality. Already, a federal district court has ordered the Arkadelphia, Arkansas, school board to stop its use of urinalysis testing of students and prohibited the board from using test results to discipline students.[26] The Arkadelphia policy had authorized schools to test any student they suspected of drug or alcohol use, whatever the reason for that suspicion, and to expel any student found to have even a trace of drugs, alcohol, paint or glue in his or her system. After a challenge by the New Jersey Civil Liberties Union, a New Jersey school district dropped a plan to give all students urine tests for drugs without any pretense of individualized suspicion as part of an annual physical. The judge ruled than even if the purpose was solely medical the test would violate the reasonable privacy expectations of children.[27] A federal court in Washington, D.C., has ruled that a school bus attendant has a reasonable expectation of privacy from search by mandatory urine testing for drugs if such testing is conducted without probable cause or individualized suspicion. The court stated that this privacy expectation outweighed public safety considerations.[28]

Can evidence obtained in an illegal search be used to prosecute or discipline a student?

A number of state courts have ruled that the exclusionary rule (that illegally obtained evidence is inadmissible in a legal proceeding) also applies when it is a school official, rather than a police officer, who has conducted the search. But most of these cases concern criminal prosecutions or delinquency proceedings. It is less clear whether the exclusionary rule applies in a school disciplinary hearing. Some courts have held that schools may not use evidence obtained in an unconstitutional search as grounds to punish students,[29] whereas other courts have reached the opposite conclusion.[30]

The chancellor of the New York City schools has applied a modified version of the exclusionary rule for school suspension hearings. Students may not be punished for an infraction based solely on the findings of an illegal search. If the charges cannot be upheld on other evidence, the student must be reinstated to the same school without a blemish on the permanent record. Cases involving weapons are treated differently, however. If an illegal search leads to the discovery of a weapon, a sealed record must be kept in the event the student is involved in new disciplinary proceedings. If no such incident occurs, the record is to be destroyed upon the student's graduation.[31] This rule balances students' right to privacy against the need to protect schools from dangerous weapons.

What are the rules governing searches by police?

Unlike school officials, police are held to the full probable cause and warrant requirements of the Fourth Amendment in schools as well as on the street.[32] If the security guards in your school have the power to make an arrest, they are viewed as police rather than as school officials for purposes of determining when they may conduct a search.[33] However, even police may make a warrantless search in an emergency when "exigent circumstances" make it likely that someone will be hurt or evidence will be destroyed if they wait for a warrant.[34] Police can also make a warrantless search of a person and areas within his or her immediate reach at the time of an arrest.[35] Police can "stop and frisk" a person without full probable cause or a warrant if the police officer has a reasonable basis to believe that there is criminal activity underway and that the suspect is armed. The search must be limited to a pat-down of outer clothing strictly for the purpose of discovering weapons.[36]

What can students do to protect themselves against searches of their persons or property?

In case of a search of your person or locker, desk, etc., the best you can do is to follow these rules:

1. Your best protection is never to carry on you or keep in school anything that you wouldn't want the police or school officials to know about for any reason.

2. Never consent to any search. Say in a loud, clear voice, so that witnesses can hear, that you do not consent. *But do not resist* if a policeman or school official goes ahead with the search. If you don't consent to the search, there's a possibility that anything found on you will not be able to be used against you in court or in disciplinary proceedings. If you consent, it may be used.

NOTES

1. New York City Chancellor's Regulation A-412, 10/1/79.
2. Cleveland Public Schools, Student Handbook.
3. *In re Christopher W.*, 29 Cal. App. 3d 777 (1973).
4. *Adams v. City of Dothan Board of Education*, 485 So.2d 757 (Ala. Civ. App. 1986); *Birdsey v. Grand Blanc Community Schools*, 344 N.W.2d 342 (Mich. App. 1983); *Boynton v. Casey*, 543 F. Supp. 995 (D. Maine 1982); *Tarter v. Raybuck*, 556 F. Supp. 625 (N.D. Ohio 1983); *Hall v. Tawney*, 621 F.2d 607 (4th Cir. 1980).
5. *New Jersey v. T.L.O.*, 105 Sup. Ct. 733, 741 (1985).
6. *Id.* at 744.
7. *State v. Mora*, 307 So.2d 317 (La.) *vacated sub. nom. Louisiana v. Mora*, 423 U.S. 809 (1975), *modified*, 330 So.2d 900 (La.), *cert. denied*, 429 U.S. 1004 (1976). See also La. Rev. Stat. Ann. §416.3.
8. *People v. D.*, 358 N.Y.S.2d 403 (Ct. App. 1974); *In re John Doe VIII v. State*, 540 P.2d 827 (N.Mex. Ct. App. 1975); *State v. McKinnon*, 558 P.2d 781 (Wash. 1977).
9. *In re William G.*, 709 P.2d 1287 (Sup. Ct. Calif. 1985).
10. *People v. D.*, *supra*.
11. *R.J.M. v. State*, 456 So. 2d 584 (Fla. 3d Dist. Ct. App. 1984).
12. *Horton v. Goose Creek Independent School Dist.*, 690 F.2d 470 (5th

    Cir. 1982); *Jones v. Latexo Independent School Dist.*, 499 F. Supp. 223 (E.D. Tex. 1980).

13. *Kuehn v. Renton School Dist.*, 694 P.2d 1078 (Wash. Sup. Ct. 1985).

14. *Bellnier v. Lund*, 438 F. Supp. 47 (N.D.N.Y. 1977).

15. *M.M. v. Anker*, 477 F. Supp. 837 (E.D.N.Y. 1979).

16. *Doe v. Renfrow*, 475 F. Supp. 1012 (N.D. Ind. 1979); *aff'd*, 631 F.2d 91 (7th Cir. 1980).

17. *Tarter v. Raybuck*, 556 F. Supp. 625 (N.D. Ohio 1983), *aff'd*, 742 F.2d 977 (6th Cir. 1984).

18. Jefferson County Public School Dist. Search Procedure, 2/9/82.

19. Richland County School Dist. Policy Rule JCAB/JCAB-R Student Searches, adopted 7/17/84.

20. *Cheney v. Mareno*, Civil Action No. C85-676 (N.D. Ohio 1980); *People v. Overton*, 301 N.Y.S.2d 479 (1969).

21. *Horton v. Goose Creek, supra.*

22. *In re William G., supra.*

23. *In re Engelrud*, 463 A.2d 934 (N.J. Sup. Ct. 1983).

24. La. Rev. Stat. Ann. §416.3.

25. Fla. Stat. §232.256; Md. Educ. Code Ann. §7-307.

26. *Anable v. Ford*, Civil Action No. 84-6033 (W.D. Ark. 7/12/85).

27. *Odenheim v. Carlstadt–East Rutherford Regional School*, 211 N.J. Super. 54 (Chancery Div. Bergen Cty. 1985).

28. *Jones v. McKenzie*, 628 F. Supp. 1500 (D.D.C. 1986).

29. *Smyth v. Lubbers*, 398 F. Supp. 777 (W.D. Mich. 1975); *Jones v. Latexo, supra.*

30. *Gordon J. v. Santa Ana Unified School Dist.*, 208 Cal. Rptr. 657 (Ct. App. 4th Dist. 1984).

31. *Matter of Renaldo F.*, Chancellor's Decision, Board of Education of City of New York, 11/23/82.

32. *Kuehn v. Renton, supra*; *Waters v. U.S.*, 311 A.2d 835 (D.C. Ct. App. 1973); *Picha v. Wieglos*, 410 F. Supp. 1214 (N.D. Ill. 1976).

33. *People v. Bowers*, 339 N.Y.S.2d 783 (Crim. Ct. 1973); *State v. Trippe*, 246 S.E.2d 122 (Ga. App. 1978).

34. *Michigan v. Tyler*, 436 U.S. 499 (1978).

35. *Chimel v. California*, 395 U.S. 752 (1969).

36. *Terry v. Ohio*, 392 U.S. 1 (1968).

VI

Corporal Punishment

What is corporal punishment and is it legal?

Corporal punishment is the infliction of physical pain or discomfort as a disciplinary measure. The term does not include situations where a school official uses force to ward off physical injury or to protect property from damage.[1]

The use of *excessive* physical force by school officials on students is illegal. The Supreme Court has ruled, however, that moderate corporal punishment in schools does not violate the Eighth Amendment's prohibition against cruel and unusual punishment.[2] Nothing in this decision prevents states, municipalities, or school districts from banning corporal punishment through statute, regulation, or written policy, and a number have done so. These include Maine, Massachusetts, New Jersey, Hawaii, and most recently New York, California, and the District of Columbia, and such cities as Atlanta, Chicago, New York, New Orleans, Pittsburgh, Providence, and San Francisco, as well as many small or rural districts.

It is significant that some of the largest school systems in the country have banned corporal punishment for many years. It is often argued that schools cannot keep order and discipline without the threat of physical force. Clearly, if large urban school systems can function without the use of corporal punishment, so can schools in small towns. The National Education Association, a nation-wide organization of teachers, has recommended the abolition of "infliction of physical pain upon students" for purposes of discipline.[3] Similarly, in 1979 the American Public Health Association announced a policy that it:

1. joins other professional organizations in opposing the use of corporal punishment in schools and all other institutions, public and private, where children are cared for or educated;

2. urges attention to the social forces and structures which cause teachers and other institution personnel to resort to corporal punishment;

3. supports the development and implementation of

programs to educate teachers in positive approaches to student discipline;

4. favors legislation comparable to that already adopted by the states of New Jersey, Massachusetts, and Hawaii and many cities, which outlaws corporal punishment of children in schools and institutions;

5. will work actively toward the passage of legislation banning corporal punishment in schools and institutions through testifying before the appropriate legislative committees, cooperating with other associations concerned with this issue, or other means consistent with the policies of the Association.[4]

What are the arguments against corporal punishment?

One argument is that corporal punishment has been prohibited for many years in the military services and, more recently, in prisons as well. In a case involving physical force inflicted on prisoners in Arkansas, the court held that the use of the strap "offends contemporary concepts of decency and human dignity and precepts of civilization."[5]

A number of other arguments were made in a statement by the Southern California Civil Liberties Union[6] before the Los Angeles Board of Education, which subsequently voted to retain the practice. The statement pointed out that corporal punishment is ineffective and serves only to generate resentment in the student: "Nobody has shown that it is in any way effective in helping the student to develop more responsible, self-disciplined behavior or even in helping other students and teachers be more secure. In fact, use of violence on such students generates rage, resentment, and hostility and may intensify the very behavior problems that triggered the punishment."

In answer to the argument that schools have insufficient resources to deal in any other way with behavioral problems than through physical force, the Civil Liberties Union stated:

The excuse of "insufficient resources" has been used to justify cruel and harsh treatment now made illegal in most institutions, such as mental hospitals, prisons, army and navy. . . . But more importantly when we talk about insufficient resources, we must ask ourselves what justifies punishing [children] if a poorly functioning social system or an unfair and inadequate tax structure fails to provide for their needs?

A variation of the above argument about resources is that we can't get rid of corporal punishment until we have provided alternatives, but so long as there is the institutionalizing of corporal punishment it will be a barrier to the development of other alternatives. Another defense of corporal punishment is that "this is the only language that some children understand." A system which allows teachers and principals to base their behavior on this perception is truly bankrupt. . . . If this is what some young people understand, it is up to the schools, which are supposed to be centers for learning and growth, to teach them a new language.

Some school officials have justified the status quo by saying parents and/or students want it. A well-known psychologist has commented on this familiar form of reasoning: "Children may ask for drugs and adults too but that doesn't mean we give it to them. Besides, while some young people through disruptive behavior seem to 'ask for punishment' these may be the very students most in need of help. [As for parents wanting corporal punishment,] schools often do not give in to parents' demands, nor should they when those demands violate principles of sound education and mental health."

Sometimes school administrators argue that abolishment of corporal punishment couldn't be achieved without staff development and extensive retraining. What a shocking comment—that complete reeducation of our educators would be necessary in order to run the schools without hitting children. Even if it were true, and for many dedicated, sensitive, and humane teachers and principals it would not be true, such an argument evades the central question that must be asked: "Is this policy good for young people?" According to nearly unanimous expert testimony, according to the most modern insights and information drawn from a variety of professional disciplines, according to informed community opinion, it is not.

May a school inflict corporal punishment on students if their parents object?

Yes. The Supreme Court has ruled that the state has a legitimate and substantial interest in maintaining discipline in school which can outweigh the parents' right to protect their child from moderate physical punishment.[7] Because allowing schools to punish students in a manner disapproved of by their parents interferes with parents' right to bring up their children as they see fit, a number of states take parental wishes into account. For example, Illinois, Georgia, and Pennsylvania permit corporal punishment unless parents specifically notify school authorities that they may not use it on their child. In Montana, parents must be notified before corporal punishment is used.[8]

Are there other limitations on the right of school officials to inflict corporal punishment on students?

Under the Supreme Court's decision in *Ingraham*, no advance notice or hearing is required *prior* to the administration of corporal punishment. The Court ruled that the student's right to sue for damages or to press criminal assault charges for excessive punishment *after* it is inflicted is adequate procedural due process. However, those states that specifically permit corporal punishment generally set limits and conditions and in some cases provide due process protections.

A common restriction is that corporal punishment may not be used unless the student is informed beforehand what behavior can lead to its use. Georgia and Nevada incorporate this requirement in state law. A second common restriction is that corporal punishment may not be the school's first recourse in the case of misbehavior. In keeping with this, Nevada discourages corporal punishment and says it should be administered "only after all other methods of discipline have proven ineffective."

Frequently, school policy requires that corporal punishment must take place in the presence of a second school official who is informed beforehand and in the student's presence of the reason for the punishment. In Florida, teachers may strike students, but only in the presence of a second adult after consultation with the principal. In Montana, the punishment must be administered in the presence of another teacher or the principal. In Washington, a school district employee must be present.

The West Virginia Supreme Court has gone further than

some other states, ruling that a student must be "given an opportunity to explain his version of the disruptive event as such an explanation may convince a fair-minded person that corporal punishment is not warranted." West Virginia also prohibits the use of whips, paddles, "or other contrivances to administer corporal punishment. The very nature of these devices is such that their use often leads to excessive force and injury."[9]

Chances are, if your school district or your state's laws explicitly permit corporal punishment, they also indicate what punishment is prohibited. For instance, both Nevada and Washington prohibit striking the student's head or face. In Pennsylvania, students cannot be required to remove clothing. In Cleveland, Ohio, the maximum punishment is "six swats applied to the posterior."

When is corporal punishment "excessive," and what can a student do about it?

Both state and federal courts have held that a student can sue a teacher who injures him or her in the course of administering corporal punishment, even when the use of physical force is legal in that state.

In an Illinois case the court held that while it had "no doubt of the right of a teacher to inflict corporal punishment in the process of enforcing discipline," the teacher might be guilty of battery if he acted "wantonly or maliciously."[10]

In cases where punishment is particularly shocking, students may also have a federal claim for violation of their constitutional rights to privacy and bodily security. The question would be "whether the force applied caused injury so severe, was so disproportionate to the need presented, and was so inspired by malice or sadism rather than a merely careless or unwise excess of zeal that it amounted to a brutal and inhumane abuse of official power literally shocking to the conscience."[11]

Students can press criminal charges against school officials who have hurt them. School authorities can discipline or even discharge school personnel for excessive use of force or for other violations of the rules governing corporal punishment.

If you hope to prove excessive force, you must show both that it was unreasonable and unnecessary under the circumstances and that you actually suffered injury. The kind of evidence that might be presented to a court includes medical reports, photographs, and testimony of witnesses; therefore, it is important to see a doctor so you will have proof of your injuries.

Use of corporal punishment can also be challenged in court if it is used in a racially discriminatory manner. Courts in Tennessee and Louisiana, for instance, have ruled that teachers are liable for damages if their striking a student was motivated by racial prejudice.[12]

Two Texas courts have concluded that racial discrimination existed where minority students were more frequently subjected to corporal punishment than were whites, and ordered schools to change their practices.[13]

NOTES

1. I. A. Hyman, E. McDowell, and B. Raines, "Corporal Punishment and Alternatives in Schools: An Overview of Theoretical and Practical Issues," *Inequality in Education*, vol. 23 (Sept. 1978), p. 5.

2. *Ingraham v. Wright*, 430 U.S. 651 (1977).

3. "Report of the Task Force on Corporal Punishment," National Education Association (1972).

4. *Discipline*, vol. 1, no. 1 (Winter 1980), p. 10.

5. *Jackson v. Bishop*, 404 F.2d 571 (8th Cir. 1968).

6. Quoted in "Corporal Punishment in the Public Schools," ACLU report (March 1972).

7. *Baker v. Owen*, 395 F. Supp. 294 (M.D.N.C., 1975), *aff'd per curiam*, 423 U.S. 907 (1975).

8. Mont. Code Ann. §20-4 3-2.

9. *Smith v. W. Va. State Board of Education*, 295 S.E.2d 680 (Sup. Ct. of App. W.Va., 1982).

10. *City of Macomb v. Gould*, 244 N.E.2d 634 (Ill. App.2d, 3rd Dist. 1969). See also *Williams v. Cotton*, 346 So.2d 1039 (Fla. App. 1977); *Eversole v. Wasson*, 398 N.E.2d 1246 (Ill. App. 1980); *McKinney v. Greene*, 379 So.2d 69 (La. App. 1980).

11. *Hall v. Tawney*, 621 F.2d 607, 611 (4th Cir. 1980).

12. *Coleman v. Franklin Parish School Board*, 702 F.2d 74 (5th Cir. 1983); *Patton v. Bennett*, 304 F. Supp. 297 (E.D. Tenn. 1969).

13. *Hawkins v. Coleman*, 376 F. Supp. 1330 (N.D. Tex. 1974); *U.S. Holley, Intervenor v. Richardson Ind. School Dist.*, 483 F. Supp. 80 (N.D. Tex. 1979).

VII

Tracking and Competency Testing

In 1954, the Supreme Court decided in *Brown v. Board of Education of Topeka, Kansas*,[1] that education must be made available for all on equal terms, and that separation of students by race was inherently unequal. Since then, civil rights activists have focused on inequities among schools. While that is still a serious concern, inequities *within* schools have become a serious problem as well.

What's wrong with tracking?

Almost every school today has some system for tracking students into ability groups. In her book *Keeping Track*, Dr. Jeannie Oakes reports on her study of school tracking practices. She finds that most schools' tracking policies are not thought out well and that most tracking has just the opposite effect from what was intended. The lower the track, the less students are taught.[2]

One noted educator described the process in these words:

> These children, by and large, do not learn because they are not being taught effectively, and they are not being taught because those who are charged with the responsibility of teaching them do not believe that they can learn, do not expect that they can learn, and do not act toward them in ways which help them to learn.[3]

Dr. Oakes points out that the common belief that students learn better when grouped with students of similar achievement levels has been disproven by "virtually mountains of research evidence indicating that homogeneous grouping doesn't consistently help *anyone* learn better." Research has also shown that tracking fosters lower self-esteem among students in low tracks, who tend as a result to have low aspirations for the future and high drop out rates.[4]

The stigma that students often feel upon being assigned to a low track—and the resulting sense of despair and hopelessness—was poignantly expressed by one who said:

> It really don't have to be the tests, but after the tests,

there shouldn't be no separation in the classes. Because, as I say again, I felt good when I was with my class, but when they went and separated us—that changed us. That changed our idea, our thinking, the way we thought about each other and turned us to enemies toward each other—because they said I was dumb and they were smart.

When you first go to junior high school you do feel something inside—it's like ego. You have been from elementary to junior high, you feel great inside. You say, well daggone, I'm going to deal with the *people* here now, I am in junior high school. You get this shirt that says Brown Junior High or whatever the name is and you are proud of that shirt. But then you go up there and the teacher says—"Well, so and so, you're in the basic section, you can't go with the other kids." The devil with the whole thing—you lose—something in you—like it just goes out of you.[5]

When is tracking discriminatory?

The placement of students in different ability groups is affected in large part by racial and socioeconomic factors; thus, white middle-class students end up in the college preparatory classes while poor and minority students end up in the slow and vocational-training classes. Sometimes this separation results from the race and class bias of those making the placements. As Dr. Oakes concludes, a teacher may have to make placement judgments on 150 or more students, a counselor on 500 or more. They could not possibly know each student well enough to make sound decisions on ability grouping and are likely to be influenced by dress, speech patterns, the way the students act toward adults, and other factors that have more to do with race and class than with ability or achievement.[6]

This problem is made worse by the tendency of schools to rely excessively on standardized tests, which are often culturally biased (that is, the questions draw on the experiences of middle-class rather than poor children). In the words of a judge who held the tracking system in Washington, D.C., to be unconstitutionally discriminatory:

Because these tests are standardized primarily on and are relevant to a white middle-class group of students, they produce inaccurate and misleading test scores when given to lower class and Negro students. As a result, rather than being classified according to ability to learn, these students are in reality being classified according to their socioeconomic or racial status, or—more precisely—according to environmental and psychological factors which have nothing to do with innate ability.[7]

A federal judge in Georgia found that even when blacks and whites got the same scores, the whites were put in higher groups.[8] In addition, students whose first language is not English may have their scores brought down by the vocabulary sections on standardized tests as well as by the tests' assumptions about attitudes and common experiences. That means their actual ability is not reflected by their scores.

Another problem with standardized tests is that they are designed on a curve, so that some students have to do worse than others. Dr. Oakes observes that when tests are being designed, the best test questions for judging reading ability are sometimes eliminated because too many students get them right. As a result, differences in scores do not necessarily mean significant differences in reading ability, yet the differences are taken very seriously when students are grouped by ability.[9] A third problem is that reading scores are often used to track students in subjects such as science or history, without consideration of their interest or aptitude for those subjects.

The inflexibility of tracking is pernicious. Once students are placed in a lower track, it is very hard to move up again. In effect, placement in a low track in school can condemn a student to a "low track" for the rest of his life, for his job possibilities upon graduation are severely limited by the kind of education he has received. As the system worked in Washington, D.C.:

Those in the lower tracks [were], for the most part, molded for various levels of vocational assignments; those in the upper tracks, on the other hand, [were] given the opportunity to prepare for the higher ranking jobs and most significantly, for college.[10]

In schools where a tracking system is particularly rigid and separation between the tracks is nearly complete, students frequently become polarized along racial or class lines. The result is tension and hostility that not only undermines the educational atmosphere, but also strengthens barriers out of school between races or classes—barriers that our society is supposedly committed to eliminating. Moreover, the consequence of separating black from white and rich from poor is that students are deprived of the educational and cultural enrichment that comes from sharing experiences with those of different backgrounds.

The connection between racial discrimination and tracking has been noted by several courts. In two cases involving recently desegregated schools, federal courts prohibited the assignment of students to classes made up of homogeneous ability groups where the result was segregated classes within the school.[11] Both courts recognized that black students had previously been forced to attend inferior schools, which caused them to score lower than white students did on the tests used as the basis for class assignments. Both courts held that until the disadvantageous effect of the inferior education previously received by black students had been eradicated, a system of heterogeneous classes would have to be maintained.

In a later case, a court again prohibited tracking because the school district failed to show that tracking would provide better educational opportunity to remedy the prior harm of segregation, especially since very few students ever moved up out of lower-track groups.[12]

Can a student challenge placement in a low track?

No court has ruled that tracking is in itself unconstitutional or a violation of equal educational opportunity. Moreover, courts are reluctant to second-guess educational decisions. Courts have, however, required hearings before students were placed outside of regular classes, and have put the burden on the school to justify its classification of the student.[13] As was discussed in chapter 8, there are numerous due process protections for students whom the school wants to classify as mentally disturbed, mentally retarded, or otherwise handicapped.

If you wish to consider a challenge to your tracking placement, you should find out the criteria used for making placements in a given track. For example, in a New York school it was discovered that one factor was the desire of school officials to have an equal number of boys and girls in each class; thus some students were placed in tracks lower than those for which their test scores qualified them.

Your chances of changing your placement are particularly strong if the track you were put in provides an entirely different type of education from the highest track, rather than the same courses on a less advanced level. If you want to be in a college preparatory course, or to qualify for certain jobs, that decision should be yours and not the guidance counselor's. You should not let anyone cut off the possibility of your going to college by putting you in a track against your will just because your grades are low, or because no one else in your family ever went to college, or for any other reason. You should demand whatever type of education you want.

What's wrong with competency tests?

Tests have long been used for tracking, but in recent years about three-fourths of the states have started using competency tests to improve schools. Often a student's graduation or promotion to the next grade depends on the results of such tests. Proponents of competency testing say it helps identify teachers and schools that need improvement, provides an incentive to students to work harder, and guarantees that when students get a diploma they have basic skills. But there are also many dangers inherent in competency testing. Teachers may teach only what is necessary to pass multiple choice tests, drilling students on facts and failing to emphasize abstract thought and creativity. Many fear that competency testing will increase the drop-out rate. Marginal students may prefer to leave school rather than fail a critical test and be labeled unintelligent.[14]

Such testing may also be discriminatory. In Florida, for instance, students were first told they would have to pass a competency test to get a high school diploma when they were already eleventh-graders. Many were blacks who had spent much of their education in inferior segregated schools. They were told that if they could not pass the competency test they would only receive certificates of attendance. This not only would have stigmatized the students but also would have resulted in fewer educational and career opportunities for them. A court was persuaded to order the state not to give the test for several years, finding that students did not have sufficient notice to pass the test as well as to meet all other diploma requirements. The court also found that the test was not instructionally valid—that is, it tested topics that students had never been taught in class. Eventually, when the court was convinced that the test reflected what was actually being taught, it permitted the test to be given.[15] A similar challenge to a standardized test used as a diploma requirement in Georgia had the same result. The test was found to be constitutionally proper since it furthered the state's interest in improving education, but the burden was on the school district to show that the content of the test was in fact taught in school.[16]

How does competency testing affect students with handicapping conditions?

Several courts have ruled that special education students could be denied regular diplomas if they were unable to pass the minimum competency tests required of all students. The highest court in New York ruled that three years' notice was enough time for schools to put together an Individualized Education Program (IEP) with remedial assistance adequate to help students pass the required tests.[17] A federal court in Georgia ruled that Section 504 of the Rehabilitation Act of 1973 does not require giving a diploma to a student who cannot pass a minimum competency test.[18]

A federal appeals court in Illinois, on the other hand, ordered the state to give several handicapped students their high school diplomas when the students were able to prove that they failed the test because they had not received the instruction they needed. The court found that a year-and-a-half notice before the test was given was not adequate, particularly since as much as 90 percent of the material covered on the test was not included in the students' educational programs. The court ruled that Section 504 required that the students' school programs take into account the work needed to pass the competency tests and that test modifications be provided so that the students' handicapping conditions would not mask their true ability to do the work.[19] Such modifications can include extended time to take the test, a less distracting test setting, a special braille or large-type version of the test, use of a calculator, etc., depending on the nature of the student's handicap. These modifications must also be included in the student's educational program.

Some states, such as New Jersey, do not require special education students to pass competency tests to earn a high school diploma. Rather, the standard is that they successfully meet the goals of their educational programs.

What happens when you can't pass the tests you need for a diploma?

Some states with minimum competency test programs build in a series of mandated skills tests in earlier grades and require schools to provide remedial help to students who fail those tests. In New York, state regulations require an "appropriate remediation plan" be sent in writing to the parent and continue until the student gets a satisfactory score on a subsequent test.[20] New Jersey requires that students be tested yearly. If they show basic skills deficiencies they must be formally assessed by the school's teaching staff and receive a medical examination. Based on that assessment, the school must develop an Individual Student Improvement Plan for the student that lists the areas where the student needs help, sets specific goals for improvement, and specifies what type of instructional program the student will receive, who will provide instruction, how often instruction will take place, and what teaching materials will be used. There must be a yearly review of the student's progress.[21]

If by the end of the eleventh grade a New Jersey student has not passed one or more parts of the competency tests needed to graduate, a Special Review Assessment is held by teachers not currently instructing the student to see whether the student actually has the required level of basic skills despite his or her inability to pass the test. If the student first entered an English-speaking school system in the ninth grade or later, the assessment must take place in his or her native language. If the student's school does not have services for students who are not proficient in English, the competency tests must be translated into the student's native language.[22]

These requirements may sound complicated, but they are supposed to guarantee that students get help to meet standards. If a testing program puts all the burden on students to meet competency standards and does not require schools to teach students what they need to know to meet these standards, it is inherently unfair.

Should students be held over if they can't pass tests?

In 1981, the New York City Board of Education passed the "Promotional Gates" policy requiring that fourth- and seventh-graders who failed standardized reading or math tests be held over in special classes and not promoted to the next grade until they passed the tests. This program was widely copied by states and cities across the country, but it was severely criticized by local parents, teachers and advocates. They noted that publishers of the test specifically warned that it was not valid for promotion decisions. They also found that two-thirds of the students held over in the first year of the program had been forced to repeat a grade at least once before, meaning that they would be much older than their classmates by the time they got to high school, and therefore more likely to drop out before they earned a diploma. The board has made changes in the program in response to such criticisms. Students are no longer held over more than once in a "Gates" grade and are not held over for low math scores. Two tests are given and students who pass either one are promoted to the next grade. If a student is slated to be held over, either the parent or the school can initiate an individual review process, considering factors such as age, handicapping conditions, class work, previous test scores, temporary problems that might have affected test performance, etc.[23]

But even when hold-over decisions are made more fairly, they may not be a good idea. The majority of researchers in the area have found that retention does not result in improved student achievement.[24] Moreover, Census Bureau data reveal that students are more likely to be retained if they are black or Hispanic, if their families are below the poverty level, or if their parent has had less than 12 years of education.[25] In other words, retention has a discriminatory impact.

School officials in Greensville County, Virginia, agreed to make extensive changes in their use of standardized tests for retention and tracking after plaintiffs in a desegregation suit against the county board claimed the practices were being used to undermine desegregation in the county.[26] In Alabama, on the other hand, a federal appeals court upheld a policy of holding students over if they were found to be reading below grade level, even though the policy affected black students more than white. The court said that ability grouping was forbidden only if it causes the resegregation of classes or schools and found that was not the case.[27]

NOTES

1. *Brown v. Board of Education of Topeka, Kansas*, 347 U.S. 483 (1954).
2. Jeannie Oakes, *Keeping Track: How Schools Structure Inequality* (New Haven, CT: Yale University Press, 1985).
3. Kenneth Clark, *Dark Ghetto* (1965).
4. Oakes, *op. cit.*, pp. 7–8.
5. Schafer et al., "Programmed for Social Class: Tracking in High School," *Transaction* (Oct. 1970).
6. Oakes, *op. cit.*, pp. 12–13.
7. *Hobson v. Hansen*, 269 F. Supp. 401 (D.D.C. 1967).
8. *Anderson v. Banks*, 520 F. Supp. 472 (S.D. Ga. 1982).
9. Oakes, *op. cit.*, pp. 12–13.
10. *Hobson v. Hansen, supra.*
11. *Moses v. Washington Parish School Board*, 330 F. Supp. 1340 (E.D. La. 1971), *aff'd*, 456 F.2d 1285 (5th Cir. 1972); *McNeal v. Tate County School District*, 508 F.2d 1017 (5th Cir. 1975).
12. *United States v. Gadsden County School District*, 572 F.2d 1049 (5th Cir. 1978).
13. *Mills v. Board of Education of the District of Columbia*, 348 F. Supp. 866 (D. D.C. 1972); *Pennsylvania Association for Retarded Children v. Commonwealth of Pennsylvania*, 334 F. Supp. 1257 (E.D. Pa. 1971).
14. D. M. Lewis, "Certifying Functional Literacy: Competency Testing and Implications for Due Process and Equal Educational Opportunity," *Journal of Law and Education*, vol. 8 (April 1979), p. 145.
15. *Debra P. v. Turlington*, 474 F. Supp. 244 (M.D. Fla. 1979), *aff'd in part, vacated and remanded in part*, 644 F.2d 397 (5th Cir. 1981), *on remand*, 564 F. Supp. 177 (M.D. Fla. 1983), *aff'd*, 730 F.2d 1405 (11th Cir. 1984).
16. *Anderson v. Banks*, 520 F. Supp. 472 (S.D. Ga. 1982), *sub. nom. Johnson v. Sikes*, 730 F.2d 644 (11th Cir. 1984).
17. *Board of Education of Northport–East Northport Union Free School District v. Ambach*, 436 N.Y.S.2d 564 (Sup. 1981), 458 N.Y.S.2d 680 (1982), 469 N.Y.S.2d 669 (Ct. App. 1983), *cert. denied*, 104 S. Ct. 1598 (1984).
18. *Anderson v. Banks, supra.*
19. *Brookhart v. Board of Education*, 534 F. Supp. 725 (C.D. Ill. 1981), *rev'd*, 697 F.2d 179 (7th Cir. 1983).

20. New York State Education Regulations, Part 100.4.

21. N.J.S.A. §§18A:4–15 *et seq.* as supplemented and amended by N.J.S.A. §§18A:7A-1 *et seq.*

22. N.J.S.A. §§18A:7C-1 *et seq.*

23. New York City Chancellor's Regulation A-501, 5/86.

24. David Larrabee, "Setting the Standard: Alternative Policies for Student Promotion," 54 *Harvard Education Review* 67 (1984).

25. Page McCullough, *New Promotion and Retention Policies: What They Mean for Children in Your Schools* (Atlantic Center for Research in Education, March 1986).

26. *Wright v. County Board of Greensville County, Va.* Civil Action No. 4263 (E.D. Va. 1981).

27. *Bester v. Tuscaloosa City Board*, Civil Action No. 82-7349 (11th Cir. 1/16/84).

VIII

Students with Handicapping Conditions

Two important federal laws guarantee every student's right to a free and appropriate public education regardless of handicap. The Education for All Handicapped Children Act (P.L. 94-142) specifies the procedures for receiving special education services and provides some federal funds to school districts in states that agree to follow those procedures.[1] Section 504 of the Rehabilitation Act of 1973[2] is a general civil rights law for disabled people which prohibits school systems from denying access to educational services on the basis of a handicap. It requires that the needs of handicapped students be met as adequately as the needs of nonhandicapped students, whether the services are provided in regular or special education classes.

Each state has statutes and regulations that govern the details of how educational services are provided to students with handicaps. State rules cannot conflict with federal law, but they can and often do provide for more services and rights than federal law requires.

Who is covered by P.L. 94-142 and Section 504?

The term "handicapped children" under P.L. 94-142 includes those who are mentally retarded, hard of hearing or deaf, blind or with impaired sight, speech-impaired, seriously emotionally disturbed, orthopedically impaired (having impairments that tend to prevent movement), or otherwise health-impaired (lacking in strength, vitality, or alertness due to a chronic or acute health problem). It also includes students with specific learning disabilities (e.g., dyslexia, an impairment of the ability to read).

Section 504 defines a handicapped person as anyone who has a physical or mental impairment that limits at least one major life activity. A physically handicapped student who does not need the special instruction provided by P.L. 94-142 still is guaranteed the same education that unimpaired students receive under Section 504 and its accompanying regulations.

P.L. 94-142 and Section 504 protect all students who, rightly or wrongly, are suspected of having a handicapping condition.

The laws can be used to prevent misclassification and mis-placement and to keep students out of special education as well as to obtain needed services. For instance, the federal regu-lations specifically state that students should not be labeled "learning-disabled" if their learning problems are primarily due to environmental, cultural, or economic disadvantage.[3] Stu-dents cannot be considered seriously emotionally disturbed unless they exhibit one or more specific signs of mental illness over a long time and to a marked degree, and unless those signs adversely affect their educational performance. A student cannot be placed in a special education program for the emo-tionally disturbed simply because he or she is "socially malad-justed."[4] To be labeled mentally retarded, the student must not only be significantly below average in intellectual func-tioning but also must show deficits in "adaptive behavior" (real-life situations).[5]

Can labeling of students be discriminatory?

Yes. Not all school districts scrupulously follow these rules and minority students continue to be grossly overrepresented in classes for the mentally retarded and emotionally handicapped.

As a result of a court challenge to discriminatory placements in programs for the emotionally disturbed, the New York City Board of Education agreed to implement a set of safeguards recommended by educational experts, including keeping a ra-cial and ethnic breakdown of referrals for special education evaluations.[6]

In a Mississippi case, plaintiffs proved that black students were disproportionately more likely to be labeled "educable mentally retarded" while white students were more likely to be labeled "learning disabled" because of overreliance on ra-cially discriminatory IQ tests. They obtained a remedial plan to change procedures and help students who had been mis-classified to make up missed work in regular classes.[7]

In California a federal court issued an order prohibiting the use of standardized IQ test results as the basis for placement in "educatable mentally retarded" classes. The court noted that even the school officials who had been sued apparently con-ceded that the tests were culturally biased, and that some school districts (New York City perhaps being the most prominent) have stopped using IQ tests altogether.[8]

Another lawsuit attacked the practice whereby some students whose primary language was not English were mistakenly placed in classes for the mentally handicapped. As a result of an agreement filed in court, all such students will have their placements reevaluated, and, in the future, appropriate testing and examination will be administered to insure that language and cultural factors will not determine school placement.[9]

Do school buildings have to be accessible to students with physical disabilities?
Yes. Section 504 requires schools to make their buildings and classes accessible to all students.[10] Buildings built after June 3, 1977, must be barrier-free. Buildings started or existing before that date must be altered so that students with physical handicaps can attend. By June 1980 all such buildings were supposed to be accessible. State laws and local building codes often contain additional requirements that schools accommodate the needs of the physically handicapped with rules about doors, stairs, public toilets, elevators, drinking fountains, public telephones, etc.

These protections mean it is illegal to require students to attend school in separate buildings because narrow doorways, lack of elevators, inaccessible bathrooms, or other physical features of the school make it hard for physically handicapped students to use the regular school building. Instead, the school must build ramps, relocate classes, or do whatever else is necessary to reasonably accommodate handicapped students.

If schools fail to meet these requirements, the mobility-impaired student can use the due process procedures of P.L. 94-142, described at the end of this chapter, or can file a complaint with the federal Department of Education's Office of Civil Rights simply by writing a letter to the appropriate regional office.[11]

The Office of Civil Rights has ordered schools to make reading labs and home economics rooms accessible, to provide accessible bathrooms and water fountains, to fix doors and stairways, and to provide equal access to showers.[12] In one case, it told a school to make a swimming pool accessible by converting a stairway to a ramp and by installing a lift device.[13] It has ruled that carrying mobility-impaired students from one place to another does not meet the requirement that facilities be readily accessible, except in "manifestly exceptional" cases.[14]

Massachusetts' state education department ordered a school either to relocate a remedial reading group attended by a physically handicapped student to the first floor, or to provide the student with an escort during fire drills.[15] Nebraska's state education department said a school district could not require an orthopedically handicapped student to attend school out of district when it was possible to make its own school accessible to the student.[16]

What is a "free appropriate public education"?

P.L. 94-142 defines "free appropriate public education" as special education and related services which:

1) Are provided at public expense, under public supervision and direction without charge.

2) Meet the standards set by the state through its educational agency.

3) Are available for students aged 3 through 21. For ages three through five and 18 through 21, states must provide services to handicapped students if they provide services to non-handicapped students of these ages, or if they provide services to other students of that age with the same disability.

4) Conform to the student's Individualized Education Program. . . .[17]

What makes an educational program "appropriate"?

The Supreme Court, in *Board of Education v. Rowley*,[18] tried to explain the term "appropriate" as it is used in the federal law. In *Rowley*, the student was able to do above average work and to pass easily from grade to grade with the services the district was already providing. The lower court found that she could do still better but for her severe hearing handicap and ordered a sign-language interpreter to help her achieve full potential. The Supreme Court disagreed, ruling that P.L. 94-142 does not require the state to maximize the potential of each handicapped child, but only to provide the student with a program "reasonably calculated to enable the child to receive educational benefits."

How many additional services are required for handicapped students must be determined on a case-by-case basis. One important factor is how well the student is doing without the disputed services. In one case where a learning disabled student was receiving poor marks and test scores, the court ordered additional services, finding they were needed for the student to receive educational benefits.[19] The opinions of experts, particularly educators, psychologists, or doctors who have worked closely with the student, will determine what program or teaching methodology is "appropriate."

Some states place higher standards on themselves than the federal law requires, through state statutes and state plans. In North Carolina, for instance, the standard is "to insure every child a fair, full opportunity to reach full potential."[20] New Jersey school districts "must provide each handicapped pupil a special education program and services according to how the pupil can best achieve educational success."[21] Massachusetts requires that districts assure the maximum possible development of handicapped students.[22] Courts have determined that in these states schools must do more than just provide some educational benefit.[23]

If the school district can come up with more than one program that is appropriate, it is allowed to choose the least expensive program, but if there is only one appropriate program, the district may not reject it on the ground of expense.[24]

What does the "least restrictive environment" requirement mean?

P.L. 94-142 requires that handicapped students be "mainstreamed," that is, placed in a regular class, if it is possible for them to receive a satisfactory education with the use of supplementary aids and supportive services. These could include outside consultation to help the regular classroom teacher meet the handicapped student's needs, additional tutoring or speech services either in or outside of the classroom, specially designed learning materials and equipment, or a health aide to take care of the student's special physical needs.[25] Sometimes handicapped students need a separate class. In that case, the law requires that they have the most contact possible with their nonhandicapped peers and that they go to a school as close as possible to their home. The possible placements listed below go from the least to the most restrictive.

- regular education with support services
- regular education with services outside the class from one period to one-half of the day
- separate special education class in a regular school with some mainstreaming (e.g., gym, lunch, extracurricular activities, music, art, vocational subjects, some academic subjects)
- special education class in a school serving only students with handicapping conditions
- residential program (as close to the student's home as possible)
- instruction in a hospital school
- home instruction

Individual cases illustrate how the least restrictive environment provision is enforced. In one case, a hearing officer ruled that a quadriplegic student who could keep up with work in a regular classroom and whose health and safety was not endangered there should not be placed in a more restrictive setting.[26] A student who tested positive for hepatitis B did not have to be placed in a hospital setting since the hygienic guidelines followed to insure medical safety in the hospital could be easily implemented in a less restrictive environment.[27] Similarly, a student with acquired immune deficiency syndrome (AIDS) was entitled to go to a regular school, rather than receive instruction at home, because neither his health nor the health of others was threatened by school attendance.[28] In a case involving a teacher with tuberculosis, the Supreme Court ruled that Section 504 prohibits a school from excluding a sick person out of fear that the sickness might be contagious. The Court said the decision on whether the teacher's condition disqualified her from teaching should be based on "the reasonable medical judgments of public-health officials." This should help students and others suffering from AIDS, because in 1985 the U.S. Public Health Service issued guidelines stating that most students and teachers afflicted with AIDS pose no risk to others.[29] In another instance, students who were able to attend school only for half a day because of their handicap were entitled to a half-day program, regardless of the extra expense of providing transportation outside of regular school hours, rather than be confined to home instruction.[30] And in a case where a student needed to be in a climate-controlled setting, the school had to install a new air-conditioning system because requiring the student to stay within a climate-controlled capsule all day was too restrictive, even though it was in a regular class.[31]

Sometimes the preference for maximum mainstreaming must be weighed against the educational benefits of a segregated setting tailor-made for students with a handicap. In some cases, courts have ruled in favor of local school placements that allowed for limited mainstreaming—e.g., lunch, recess, library, and physical education—rather than a segregated site with a stronger academic program.[32] But in other cases courts found more restrictive settings were necessary to enable students to make any educational progress at all.[33]

How do you find out if you need special education services?
A student can be referred for a special education evaluation by a parent, teacher, school administrator, or outside agency. The evaluation cannot be made without the parent's written consent unless the school goes through an impartial hearing to overrule the parent's objection. When a referral is made, parents must be notified in writing of the reason and of their rights and their children's rights. The notice must be in the parent's primary language. Parents who are blind, deaf, or unable to read must be notified in a way they can understand. Schools cannot refer students on the basis of a single test, incident, or discussion. Evaluations must be in a student's native language and must take into account the student's handicap. For instance, schools cannot give oral aptitude tests to deaf children.[34]

If the parent disagrees with the evaluation or if the school district does not have employees qualified to test the student in his or her native language, the school system must pay for an independent evaluation performed by qualified evaluators who are not school district employees. However, the school system may instead ask for an impartial hearing to show that its own evaluation was adequate. If the school district wins the hearing, it is relieved of the obligation to pay for an independent evaluation, but the parent and student are still entitled to one if they wish. The family may also ask for an independent evaluation at the outset if they do not believe that school employees would do an adequate and unbiased job. Upon request, the school system must give the parents the names of professionals in the community who could do the evaluation.[35]

What is an "Individualized Education Program"?

If the evaluators conclude that the student needs special education services, an Individualized Education Program (IEP) must be prepared within 30 days of the completion of the evaluation.[36] (Some states require that the evaluation be completed in a shorter time.) Participants in the decision making and the development of the IEP must include one or both parents, at least one of the student's teachers, a special educator, a member of the evaluation team if the student has just been evaluated for the first time, and the student "where appropriate."[37]

The IEP sets learning goals and indicates what educational and related services will be provided to accomplish these goals, as well as how the student will be mainstreamed with non-handicapped children. The school system is legally obligated to provide whatever is included on the IEP.[38]

What related services can be required on the IEP?

Related services can include, but are not limited to, speech or hearing services, physical or occupational therapy, counseling or psychological services, social work, parent counseling and training, artistic, musical, or dance therapy, or recreation. Medical services can be required on the IEP if the handicapped student needs the services in order to benefit from his or her educational program. Physician's services can be required only for diagnostic purposes.[39] Examples of services that can be required are catheterization by a school nurse or health aide, intermittent monitoring of a student's respirator, and suction of mucus from a student's respiratory tract.

Do students with handicapping conditions have a right to participate in extracurricular activities and physical education?

Handicapped students are entitled to appropriate physical education programs. They must be given the opportunity to participate in the school's regular physical education program unless their IEP states otherwise or they are enrolled full time in a special education school.[40]

Federal regulations require that handicapped students be

given an equal opportunity to participate in nonacademic and extracurricular activities.[41] However, a federal court recently denied an autistic student's request for extracurricular activities, ruling that the school district does not have to make every special service available to handicapped children that it provides to non-handicapped children.[42] Courts have also denied students with impaired hearing or sight the right to participate in contact sports where the school's decision not to let the students play was based on medical advice and "was a valid exercise of judgment and was not arbitrary or capricious."[43] On the other hand, an emotionally disturbed student who had to transfer before his last year of high school because of difficulties with his parents was allowed to play on a sports team at his new school, even though he would ordinarily not have been eligible under league rules. The court ruled that the student was entitled to special consideration of individual needs under Section 504.[44]

When can students participate in IEP conferences?

The comments to the federal regulations say that it is up to the parent to decide when it is appropriate for the student to attend. The comments note that the parents and the local educational agency should encourage older handicapped children, particularly those at the secondary school level, to participate in the meetings.[45] Special education advocates can point to many occasions where the presence of the student has made a great deal of difference. In one case, a young student being considered for a class for the educable mentally retarded was asked by team members why he was behind in school. He explained that he could not see the blackboard. An eye exam revealed that his learning problem was visual. Often, attending an IEP conference simply helps a student understand his or her situation better. For example, a 16-year-old girl who was allowed to attend an IEP meeting finally understood that she was being evaluated not because everyone thought she was "crazy," but because she had an unusual learning disability.[46]

What are your rights if you are not satisfied with the decisions?

Parents always have the right to an impartial hearing whenever they are dissatisfied with a special education evaluation or program. It is usually wise first to discuss the issue with the school, the evaluation team, or the special education super-visor. It is also helpful to seek advice and, where possible, representation from legal services offices or special education advocacy groups, or to ask the student's doctor or therapist to intervene with school authorities. Parents of other handicapped students are a good source of advice and support, and many groups provide help to students with specific disabilities.[47] It is important to ask for and keep a complete set of the student's special education records, to keep all letters and notices, and to take written notes on all phone calls and meetings.

The fact that parental consent is necessary for the initial evaluation and placement is an important bargaining chip. If, for example, the evaluation team finds the student is learning-disabled and wants to recommend a separate special education class, a parent may decide to refuse to give consent for anything more restrictive than a resource room one or two periods a day with special assistance to the student's regular classroom teacher, on the grounds that this is a less restrictive alternative. The school district would have to ask for an impartial hearing to override the parent's objection to the separate class. In many cases, school officials will prefer to try it the parent's way first.

If the school authorities want to change the student's place-ment or IEP *after* he or she is in special education, they need only consult with and notify the parent. If parents want to maintain the status quo—that is, prevent a change in the stu-dent's special education program—it is their responsibility to request an impartial hearing. Likewise, if the parents want services different from those the team is willing to put in the IEP, it is up to the parents to request the hearing.

How do I get an impartial hearing?

To initiate a hearing, parents need only write to the local school official requesting a hearing and briefly stating their complaint. The school district must make the arrangements and make sure the hearing takes place within 45 days of the parent's request. The hearing officer must be impartial and cannot work for the school district or any other agency re-sponsible for educating or caring for the student. The school system must notify the parent of free or low-cost legal services and other relevant assistance if the parent requests the infor-mation or if the hearing is initiated by the school system.

Parents have the right to bring the student who is the subject of the hearing and to have the hearing open to the public if they wish. All parties at the hearing have the right to be accompanied and advised by counsel or by special education specialists, to present evidence, to subpoena witnesses, to cross-examine witnesses, to obtain a written or taped transcript of the complete proceedings, and to obtain written findings of fact and decision. The parent is entitled to a decision within 45 days after the request for a hearing was received.[48]

The hearing officer is not limited to accepting or rejecting the school's program. He or she can order the school to provide whatever is needed for the student, including a new program or paying for a private school.

The hearing officer's decision is final unless one of the parties appeals to the state education agency. (Such an appeal is not possible if the initial hearing was conducted by the state department of education.) The rules of your state's education department will indicate the procedure for bringing such an appeal. The state official examines the hearing record to determine whether the procedures at the hearing were consistent with the requirements of due process. The official can seek additional evidence if necessary and give all parties an opportunity for oral or written argument. The official must render a decision within 30 days of receipt of the request for review. That decision is final unless a party brings a court action. Families can bring court actions without going through the hearing and appeal process if they can show it would be useless to do so because the process itself is biased or otherwise not in conformity with law.

During the course of administrative or court proceedings, the student must stay in his or her present educational setting unless parents and school authorities agree on a different setting.

A recent federal law grants parents attorney's fees if they are represented in a hearing, appeal, or court case brought under P.L. 94-142 if they win. This should make it easier for parents to find representation.

Can special education students be suspended or expelled?
Once students have been evaluated and found to have a handicapping condition, they enjoy all the protections of P.L. 94–142. Handicapped students can be temporarily suspended

in an emergency, with the same due process protections available to regular education students.[49] Federal regulations permit a school to use "its normal procedures for dealing with children who are endangering themselves or others."[50]

Expulsions and long-term suspensions are considered to be changes of placement under P.L. 94–142, which provides students special due process protections, including the right to remain where they are while they pursue their due process rights. This would apply to any suspension longer than 10 days.[51]

Courts have held that students cannot be expelled for behavior that is caused by their handicapping condition. In one case, a school board attempted to expel a 14-year-old learning-disabled boy for acting as a "go-between" for two girls who asked him to purchase "speed" for them from a fellow student. The court found that the boy's learning disability resulted in a lack of self-esteem and that the frequent ridicule of other students made him "particularly susceptible to peer pressure." The court also concluded that the learning disability "prevented him from comprehending or giving long term consideration to the consequences of his actions."[52] His expulsion was found to be unlawful. A similar case involving emotionally handicapped students is now being reviewed by the U.S. Supreme Court.[53]

The determination of whether disciplinary infractions are the result of the student's handicapping condition must be made initially by the multidisciplinary evaluation team, and its findings can be challenged in an impartial hearing. If it finds the behavior is the result of the student's handicapping condition, the student cannot be expelled but can be moved to a more restrictive setting.[54] This is also a change of placement, so if the parents and student disagree with the change the student is entitled to stay in his or her present placement during an appeal. (A more restrictive setting is not always required. For instance, in the case discussed above, everyone agreed that the student's placement was appropriate even if his behavior was not.) Some courts have ruled that if it is determined that the behavior is not related to the handicapping condition, the student can be expelled[55] but must still receive instruction—in a private or alternative school, for example, or at home.[56] The comments to the federal regulations state:

It should be stressed that, where a handicapped child is so disruptive in a regular classroom that the education of other students is significantly impaired, the needs of the handicapped child cannot be met in that environment. Therefore, regular placement would not be appropriate to his or her needs.[57]

Since this would be a change to a more restrictive setting, the student is entitled to the due process protections of P.L. 94–142. Before the recommendation for a separate class is made, the school must try to help the student improve his or her behavior through the school's normal guidance and discipline practices.[58]

One court ruled that handicapped students could be expelled for the same reasons as nonhandicapped students if the evaluation team found that their conduct was not related to their handicapping conditions. However, before such an expulsion could go into effect, the students would be entitled to exhaust the full range of administrative and court proceedings to challenge the evaluation team's decisions.[59]

The rules governing special education suspensions could change once the U.S. Supreme Court case referred to above is decided.

NOTES

1. 20 U.S.C. §§1401 *et seq*.
2. 29 U.S.C. §794.
3. 34 C.F.R. §300.5(b)(9).
4. 34 C.F.R. §300.5(b)(8)(ii).
5. 34 C.F.R. §300.5(b)(4).
6. *Lora v. Board of Education*, 587 F. Supp. 1572 (E.D.N.Y. 1984)
7. *Mattie T. v. Holladay*, Civil Action No. DC 75-31-S (N.D. Miss. 5/18/81).
8. *Larry P. v. Riles*, 343 F. Supp. 1306 (N.D. Calif. 1972), *aff'd*, 502 F.2d 963 (9th Cir. 1974); Civil Action No. 80-4027 (9th Cir. 1/28/84).
9. *Guadalupe Organization, Inc. v. Tempe Elementary School District*, Civil Action No. 71-435 PHX (D. Ariz. 1/24/72).
10. 34 C.F.R. §§104.22—104.23.

11. 34 C.F.R. §§100.8—110.10, 104.36, 104.61.

12. *Penna*, Educ. for Hand. L. Rep. (CRR), 254:03 (1978); *New Carlisle–Bethel Local School Dist.*, Educ. for Hand. L. Rep. (CRR), 257:474 (Ohio 1984); *Dixie School Dist.*, Educ. for Hand. L. Rep. (CRR), 257:474 (Calif. 1983).

13. *Coates*, Educ. for Hand. L. Rep. (CRR), 254:10 (1980).

14. OCR Policy Interpretation No. 4, Educ. for Hand. L. Rep. (CRR), 254:10 (1980).

15. *Case No. 84-0094*, Educ. for Hand. L. Rep. (CRR), 505:413 (Mass. 1984).

16. *Case No. 83-05*, Educ. for Hand. L. Rep. (CRR), 505:246 (Nebr. 1984).

17. 20 U.S.C. §1401(18).

18. *The Board of Education of the Hendrick Hudson School Dist. v. Rowley*, 458 U.S. 176 (1982).

19. *Blazejewski v. Board of Education of the Allegheny Central School Dist.*, 560 F. Supp. 701 (W.D.N.Y. 1983).

20. *Harrell v. Wilson*, 293 S.E.2d 687 (N.C. App. Ct. 1982).

21. *Geis v. Board of Education of Parsippany–Troy Hills*, 589 F. Supp. 269 (D. N.J. 1984), *aff'd*, 774 F.2d 575 (3d Cir. 1985).

22. *Town of Burlington v. Dept. of Education*, 136 F.2d 773 (1st Cir. 1984); *David D. v. Dartmouth*, 615 F. Supp. 639 (D. Mass 1984), *aff'd*, Civil Action No. 84-1937 (1st Cir. 10/15/85), *cert. denied*, 106 S. Ct. 1790 (1986).

23. Courts have ruled that because state standards for appropriateness are incorporated by reference in P.L. 94–142, they are enforceable by federal courts. See *Burlington*, 736 F.2d at 789; *Geis*, 744 F.2d at 580.

24. *Armstrong v. Kline*, 476 F. Supp. 583 (E.D. Pa. 1979).

25. 20 U.S.C. §1412(5)(B).

26. *Case No. 10610*, Educ. for Hand. L. Rep. (CRR), 502:350 (N.Y. 1981).

27. *Case No. SE 837*, Educ. for Hand. L. Rep. (CRR), 504:371 (Calif. 1983).

28. *Board of Education of the City of Plainfield v. Cooperman*, 517 A.2d 436 (N.J. Sup. Ct. 1986); *In re Ryan W.*, Educ. for Hand. L. Rep. (CRR), 507:239 (Ind. 1985). See also *Case No. 84–20*, Educ. for Hand. L. Rep. (CRR), 507:303 (Ct. 1985); *District 27 Community School Board v. Board of Education*, Index. No. 14940/85 (Sup. Ct. Queens Cty. 2/11/86), Educ. for Hand. L. Rep. (CRR), 557:241 (N.Y. 1986).

29. *School Board of Nassau County v. Arline*, 107 S.Ct. 1123 (1987), rehearing denied, 107 S.Ct. 1913.

30. *In re I.S.D.*, No. 625, Educ. for Hand. L. Rep. (CRR), 503:176 (Minn. 1981).

31. *Espino v. Besteiro*, 520 F. Supp. 905 (S.D. Tex. 1981).

32. *Roncker on Behalf of Roncker v. Walter*, 700 F.2d 1058 (6th Cir. 1983).

33. *St. Louis Developmental Disabilities Treatment Center Parents Association v. Mallory*, 591 F. Supp. 1416 (W.D. Mo. 1984), *aff'd*, 767 F.2d 518 (8th Cir. 1985).

34. 34 C.F.R. §300.505(b).

35. 34 C.F.R. §300.503.

36. 34 C.F.R. §300.343(c).

37. 34 C.F.R. §300.344(a).

38. 34 C.F.R. §300.346. For a clear discussion of the contents of the I.E.P., see Children's Defense Fund, *94-142 and 504: Numbers That Add Up to Educational Rights for Handicapped Children* (1984).

39. *Irving Independent School District v. Tatro*, 468 U.S. 883 (1984).

40. 34 C.F.R. §300.307.

41. 34 C.F.R. §300.306.

42. *Rettig v. Kent City School District*, 720 F.2d 463, 788 F.2d 328 (6th Cir. 1986), *cert. denied*, 467 U.S. 1257 (1986).

43. *Colombo v. Sewanhaka Central H.S. Dist. No. 2*, 383 N.Y.S.2d 518 (S.Ct. Nassau Cty. 1976); *Kampmeier v. Nyquist*, 553 F.2d 296 (2d Cir. 1977).

44. *Doe v. Marshall*, 459 F. Supp. 1190 (S.D. Tex. 1978), cert. denied, 462 U.S. 1119 (1983).

45. 46 Fed. Reg. 5461 (1/19/81).

46. D. Pullin, *Special Education: A Manual for Advocates* (Center for Law and Education, 1982) at 4/7.

47. See Children's Defense Fund, *supra*, for list of advocacy organizations.

48. 34 C.F.R. §§300.506–300.510, 300.512.

49. *Kaelin v. Grubbs*, 682 F.2d 595 (6th Cir. 1982); *Stuart v. Nappi*, 443 F. Supp. 1235 (D. Conn. 1978); *Board of Education of the City of Peoria v. Illinois State Board of Education*, 531 F. Supp. 148 (C.D. Ill. 1982).

50. 34 C.F.R. §300.513.

51. *S-1 v. Turlington*, 635 F.2d 342 (5th Cir. 1981), *cert. denied*, 454 U.S. 1030 (1981); *School Board of the County of Prince Williams, Va. v. Malone*, 762 F.2d 1210 (4th Cir. 1985); *Kaelin v. Grubbs, supra*; *Stuart v. Nappi, supra*; *Sherry v. New York State Education Department*, 479 F. Supp. 1328 (W.D.N.Y. 1979); *Doe v. Koger*, 480 F. Supp. 225 (N.D. Ind. 1979).

52. *Jackson v. Franklin County School Board*, 606 F. Supp. 152 (S.D.

Miss. 1985), *aff'd* 765 F.2d 535 (5th Cir. 1985); *Victoria L. v. Connecticut School Board*, 741 F.2d 989 (11th Cir. 1981).

53. *Doe v. Maher*, 793 F.2d 1470 (9th Cir. 1986), *cert. granted*, in part, *Honig v. Doe*, 107 S.Ct. 1284 (1987).

54. *Doe v. Koger, supra.*

55. *School Board of the County of Prince Williams, Va., supra*, at 1218.

56. *Stuart v. Nappi, supra.*

57. 34 C.F.R. §300.552.

58. *Lamont v. Quisenberry*, 606 F. Supp. 809 (S.D. Ohio, 1984).

59. *Doe v. Maher, supra.*

IX

Sex Discrimination

It should go without saying that you have a right not to be discriminated against in school on the basis of race, religion, or ethnic background. Racial segregation within the public schools has been a major political and legal concern of the nation since 1954, when, in the case of *Brown v. Board of Education*, the Supreme Court ruled that separate schools for different races were by definition not equal and that segregated public schools were therefore in violation of the equal protection clause of the Fourteenth Amendment. Hundreds of cases involving different aspects of school segregation—*de facto* segregation, racial imbalance, freedom of choice, busing, token integration, housing patterns—have gone to the courts since that landmark decision, and most decisions have clarified or extended the right of students to integrated schooling. The matter, unfortunately, is still not settled and will not be for many years to come.

If you feel that you are meeting discrimination in your school because of your race, ethnic background, or religion, you should take the matter to a community group that focuses on such problems or to a lawyer knowledgeable in segregation cases.

The Fourteenth Amendment and various state and federal laws also prohibit schools from discriminating against students on the basis of sex. In Title IX of the Education Amendments of 1972, Congress prohibited all types of sex discrimination in educational programs that receive federal funds.[1] Because most public school programs do not receive federal funds, Title IX does not directly apply to them. Instead, a challenge to sex discrimination in a public school would have to be made on constitutional grounds. The provisions of Title IX are still important to public school students because it is unlikely that any court would uphold as constitutional a practice specifically outlawed by Title IX. What follows, therefore, is the law under both Title IX and the Constitution.

Can a public school have fixed quotas for girls and boys?
No. Title IX prohibits sex quotas. Federal courts have also

held that this practice constitutes discrimination on the basis
of sex. A Boston school that required an entrance examination
had fixed numbers of seats for boys and girls, as a result of
which the boys' scores were measured against boys' and the
girls' against girls'. Consequently some boys were admitted
with lower scores than those achieved by some girls who were
not admitted. The court held that all applicants had to be
measured against each other and those with the highest grades
had to be admitted regardless of sex.[2] A California court held
in a similar case that the use by a school of higher admission
standards for female applicants than for male applicants violates
the Fourteenth Amendment.[3]

May girls be prohibited from taking "boys'" courses such as shop and vice versa?

No. Title IX provides that no educational institution receiving federal funds may discriminate against students on the basis
of sex. This law has been interpreted by the Department of
Education, the agency which administers the law, to mean that
a school "shall not provide any course or otherwise carry out
any of its education program or activity separately on the basis
of sex, or require or refuse participation therein by any of its
students on such basis. . . ."

Are schools permitted to maintain single-sex athletic teams?

During the past decade there has been much litigation on
this question, although no case has yet reached the Supreme
Court. The issue is complicated, given the average physiological differences between males and females and the fact that
in the past females have been actively excluded from participating in competitive sports. As a result of that exclusion,
females have been at a disadvantage which the law is attempting
to remedy.

Federal regulations interpreted Title IX to provide that "no
person shall, on the basis of sex, be excluded from participation
in, be denied the benefits of, be treated differently from another
person or otherwise be discriminated against in any interscholastic, intercollegiate, club or intramural athletics offered
by [a school] and no school shall provide any athletics separately
on such basis." Exceptions are made in the regulations for

contact sports and situations in which teams are formed on the basis of competitive skill. In the latter case, if members of both sexes have been permitted to try out for the team, and it turns out that the best athletes are all boys, separate teams may be maintained.

In cases brought under the Fourteenth Amendment, courts have almost invariably upheld separate teams for boys and girls when schools provide opportunities in the particular sport for both sexes.[4] Where no alternative competitive sports programs for girls were provided by the school, and where the girls in question could compete effectively on the boys' teams, they could not be prohibited from doing so on the basis of sex.[5]

The courts have recognized that while physiological differences between males and females may prevent most girls from competing on an equal level with the majority of boys, this fact does not justify a rule against all females participating in sports with males without taking into consideration the capabilities of the individual girl.

Two cases, applying state equal rights amendments, have gone further than the federal courts in striking down sex discrimination in athletics. A Pennsylvania court and the Washington Supreme Court, in declaring unconstitutional regulations prohibiting girls from competing against boys in athletic competition, said that qualified girls have a right to compete on boys' teams even when separate girls' teams are maintained and even in contact sports.[6] Responding to the argument that "girls as a whole are weaker and thus more injury-prone, if they compete with boys, especially in contact sports," the Pennsylvania court observed:

If any individual girl is too weak, injury-prone, or unskilled, she may, of course, be excluded from competition on that basis but she cannot be excluded solely because of her sex without regard to her relevant qualifications.

A somewhat different rule has emerged for boys who wish to participate on girls' teams. In this situation, courts have upheld the exclusion of males from female teams even when no separate male team existed as long as the overall athletic opportunities for males were equal to or better than those for females.[7] The disparity in the rules for males and females has been justified by the courts' wish to remedy past discrimination against females and to insure for them extra opportunities to participate in athletics.

Are all-male or all-female public schools permissible?

It is clear that if a school offers a special program that cannot be obtained in another school, it is illegal to exclude members of either sex from that school.[8] The fact that more men than women have in the past become engineers is not, for example, a legally acceptable reason for excluding women from a technical school or for the school's taking a higher proportion of male applicants.

Whether "separate but equal" public schools for males and females are permissible is not entirely clear. An equally divided Supreme Court (Justice William Rehnquist not participating in the decision) affirmed without opinion the ruling of a Pennsylvania court that, where a school district maintained two academically superior single-sex schools, one for boys and one for girls, the exclusion of members of one sex from a school was not illegal. The Court reasoned that any disadvantages of such a system would fall equally on the members of each sex and, therefore, was not unlawful discrimination.[9]

Subsequently, however, the full Supreme Court ruled that the exclusion of a man from an all-female state nursing school violated his constitutional right to equal protection of the laws despite the fact that the state system also included coed nursing schools.[10] In rejecting the state's argument that an all-female school was permissible as an attempt to remedy past discrimination against women, the Court noted that nursing has traditionally been a female profession and no such remedial action was necessary. The Court left open the question whether an all-female school might be upheld for legitimate affirmative action purposes. The Court also found that the fact that males were permitted to audit courses at the nursing school fatally undermined the state's argument that an all-female school is justified by the adverse effect on women of men in the classroom.

Thus, while it is not entirely certain how a court would rule on single-sex schools in a given situation, the law is clear that before a court will uphold discrimination on the basis of sex, the government must produce an "exceedingly persuasive justification" for it. Increasingly, justifications traditionally relied on are becoming less persuasive.

NOTES

1. 20 U.S.C. §1681.
2. *Bray v. Lee*, 337 F. Supp. 934 (D. Mass. 1972).
3. *Berkelman v. San Francisco Unified School District*, 501 F.2d 1264 (9th Cir. 1974).
4. *O'Connor v. Board of Education of School District No. 23*, 645 F.2d 578 (7th Cir. 1981); *Bucha v. Illinois High School Association*, 351 F. Supp. 69 (N.D. Ill. 1972).
5. *Brendan v. Independent School District 742*, 477 F.2d 1292 (8th Cir. 1973); *Bednar v. Nebraska School Activities Association*, 531 F.2d 922 (8th Cir. 1976); *Hoover v. Meiklejohn*, 430 F. Supp. 164 (D. Colo. 1977); *Carnes v. Tennessee Secondary School Athletic Association*, 415 F. Supp. (E.D. Tenn. 1976).
6. *Commonwealth of Pa. v. Pennsylvania Interscholastic Athletic Assn.*, 334 A.2d 839 (Commonwealth Ct. of Pa. 1975); *Darrin v. Gould*, 540 P.2d 882 (Wash. 1975).
7. *Clark v. Arizona Interscholastic Association*, 695 F.2d 1126 (9th Cir. 1982).
8. *Kirstein v. Rector and Visitors of University of Virginia*, 309 F. Supp. 184 (E.D. Va. 1970).
9. *Vorchheimer v. School District of Philadelphia*, 532 F.2d 880 (3d Cir. 1976), *aff'd* by an equally divided court, 430 U.S. 703 (1977).
10. *Mississippi University for Women v. Hogan*, 458 U.S. 718 (1982).

X

Marriage, Pregnancy, Parenthood

It is common practice for schools to prohibit students from attending school or participating in extracurricular activities when they get married or become pregnant or have children. These rules frequently curtail the education of such students at a time when it is most crucial for many of them to continue going to school.

Now, however, as a result of federal legislation and a number of good court decisions, all such rules are illegal. The federal law is Title IX of the Education Amendments of 1972, which prohibits sex discrimination in any educational program or activity receiving federal financial assistance.[1] This law has been interpreted by the Department of Education, which administers it, to prohibit discrimination on the basis of pregnancy and marital status as well.

As discussed in the chapter on sex discrimination, it is virtually certain that a court deciding a constitutional challenge to discrimination based on pregnancy or marital status would apply the Title IX standards. This is particularly true of discrimination based on pregnancy, which numerous courts in other contexts have held to amounts to sex discrimination per se.[2]

School administrators advance a variety of reasons for their policies penalizing married and pregnant students, but in most cases the true reason turns out to be a moral one: the officials don't want students knowing or thinking or talking about sex. If a young married man is permitted to continue to play on the high school football team, they say, he may tell his teammates in the locker room about his sexual relations with his wife. Some school officials fear that if students see a pregnant classmate in school—particularly if she is unmarried—they may become morally contaminated; and as one school official so delicately put it, he wouldn't want students to think the school condoned "conduct on the part of unmarried students of a nature to cause pregnancy."[3]

Clearly these ideas are considerably outdated. The average high school student today is constantly exposed to books, movies, and magazines full of explicit sexual material, which makes it rather unlikely that a locker room conversation or the sight of a pregnant girl would have any effect at all. It is impossible for schools to protect students from sexual knowledge, whether vicarious or firsthand. Courts are beginning to recognize this fact.

Do students have a right to continue going to school if they get married?

Yes. Courts have interpreted the Constitution as prohibiting discrimination against students on the basis of marital status.

As early as 1929, a court in Mississippi held that a high school could not expel a student for getting married.[4] Thirty-five years later a Kentucky court held that there was "no reason to suppose that the marriage of a student would diminish the need of that student for an education—indeed, just the contrary would appear the case."[5] In Texas a state court ordered a married couple[6] and a married girl[7] reinstated in school upon finding that none of them had been found guilty of "incorrigible" or improper conduct by getting married.

It is not entirely clear under the Department of Education regulations whether under Title IX married students may be treated differently from nonmarried students, or whether regulations concerning married students must simply apply equally to males and females. It appears more likely, however, that under Title IX, as under the Constitution, married students of both sexes must be treated the same as other students. The regulations bar any preadmission inquiry into a student's marital status, for one thing, and for another, since discrimination against pregnant students is prohibited under Title IX, it would be anomalous to have a ruling barring married pregnant students from classes while permitting unmarried pregnant students to attend.

Do pregnant girls have a right to attend school?

Yes. The Department of Education regulations interpreting Title IX provide that a school may not discriminate against a student on the basis of her pregnancy, childbirth, false pregnancy, termination of pregnancy, or recovery therefrom unless the student requests voluntarily to participate in a separate program. If a student does make such a request, the quality of the special program must be equivalent to that of the regular program. Title IX makes no distinction between married and unmarried students.

Can students who have children attend school?

Students who are parents, married or unmarried, have both Title IX and a number of court cases backing up their right to stay in school.

In 1929 a court in Kansas ruled that a married student with a child had a right to attend high school if she wished. The court stated:

> The public schools are for the benefit of children within school age, and efficiency ought to be the sole object of those charged with the power and privilege of managing and conducting the same; and while great care should be taken to preserve order and proper discipline, it is proper also to see that no one within school age should be denied the privilege of attending school unless it is clear that the public interest demands the expulsion of such pupils or a denial of his right to attend.[8]

Forty years later, a federal court reached the same conclusion and ordered Mississippi school officials to readmit two unmarried mothers to high school unless the officials could show in a fair hearing that the young women were "so lacking in moral character that their presence in the schools [would] taint the education of other students."[9] The court held that the mere fact that a girl has borne a child out of wedlock "does not forever brand her as a scarlet woman undeserving of any chance for rehabilitation or the opportunity for future education." The court came to this conclusion even though it believed that an unmarried mother had committed "a wrong." No mention was made of unwed fathers.[10]

A Texas court ordered the admission of a young mother to high school simply on the grounds that she was entitled to an education under a state law furnishing school funds for people of her age.[11]

Do married students, pregnant students, and students with children have the right to participate in extracurricular activities?

School officials frequently argue that while attending school may be a right, participating in extracurricular activities is a privilege from which students can be arbitrarily barred. This argument would seem to have little merit in view of the court decisions finding extracurricular activities to be an essential aspect of education and in view of the well-established legal principle that even privileges cannot be denied by the state arbitrarily.

Title IX prohibits sex discrimination in any educational program or activity, which includes extracurricular activities. Further, under the Fourteenth Amendment, almost without exception, recent court decisions have declared illegal rules that penalize students who are pregnant, married, or have children.

A federal court in Illinois ordered the reinstatement in the National Honor Society of a pregnant and subsequently married student who had been dismissed from membership for deficiency of leadership and character, allegedly because of her premarital pregnancy. The court found that she had been discriminated against on the basis of sex in violation of both Title IX and the Fourteenth Amendment.[12]

A federal court in Tennessee held that the rule excluding a married girl student from all school activities except classes infringed on her right to an education. Since marriage was legal and consonant with the public policy of Tennessee, the court said, school officials could not punish a student for her married status.[13] This was also the reasoning of a court in Ohio.[14]

An Indiana court refused to accept several justifications presented by school officials for their policy of excluding married students from interscholastic sports.[15] To the argument that married students should spend their time discharging family economic responsibilities instead of playing sports, the court replied that this reason might or might not be justified for both married and unmarried students. Furthermore, the court said, a married man is presumed to be mature enough to make the proper decisions concerning his family responsibilities by himself. As for sex talk in the locker room, the court pointed out that if such talk were going to take place, there were many other opportunities for it, since married students were not segregated at any other point during the school day.

The same conclusion was reached by a Montana federal court,

which held that school officials could not prohibit a married student from playing on the high school football team, thereby depriving him of the chance to win a college scholarship. The court found that the school officials had not presented sufficient evidence to show that married students' participation in extracurricular activities would result in a reasonable likelihood of "moral pollution, disruption or disciplinary problems" within the student body.[16]

Recognizing that a student's record of participation in extracurricular activities often influences his or her ability to get into college, a Texas court ordered school officials to permit a divorced student who had put her child up for adoption to participate in extracurricular activities.[17] A New Jersey federal court has also enjoined school officials from discriminating against students with respect to participation in extracurricular activities solely on the basis of their marital or parental status.[18] The Idaho attorney general has issued an opinion declaring that marriage alone is not a reason for barring students from extracurricular activities.[19]

Do pregnant students have the right to attend graduation?

In New York State, the education commissioner overrode the decision of a local board of education to prohibit a married pregnant student from attending her high school graduation. He held that decision to be "clearly arbitrary, capricious and unreasonable" since the young woman had met all of the academic requirements.[20]

The point to stress in any dispute with school officials involving pregnancy or marital or parental status is that the burden is on them to show the rational relationship between the regulation and the functioning of the school. If no such relationship can be shown, as is usually the case, the exclusion violates your right under the Fourteenth Amendment not to be arbitrarily and capriciously deprived of an education. The HEW regulations under Title IX do not mention graduation, but it is probable that a court would consider graduation to be an educational activity under Title IX.

Do married students, pregnant students and students with children have a right *not* to attend school?

Yes. Most school systems will allow students who are married, pregnant, or have children to drop out of school, even though they are under the compulsory-attendance age. Where schools have refused to grant such permission, courts have decided in favor of letting the students leave school.[21]

NOTES

1. 20 U.S.C. §1681.
2. P.L. 95-555 is referred to as the Pregnancy Discrimination Act; its principal provision is found in §701(k) of Title VII, 42 U.S.C. §2000. See guidelines in Appendix to 29 C.F.R. Part 1604.
3. *Ordway v. Hargraves*, 323 F. Supp. 1155 (D. Mass. 1971).
4. *McLeod v. State*, 154 Miss. 468, 122 So. 737 (1929).
5. *Kentucky Board of Education of Harrodsburg v. Bentley*, 383 S.W.2d 677 (Ky. 1964).
6. *Carrollton-Farmers Branch Independent School District v. Knight*, 418 S.W.2d 535 (Tex. Ct. of Civ. App. 1967).
7. *Anderson v. Canyon Independent School District*, 412 S.W.2d 387 (Tex. Ct. of Civ. App. 1967).
8. *Nutt v. Board of Education*, 128 Kans. 507, 278 P. 1065 (1929).
9. *Perry v. Grenada Municipal Separate School District*, 300 F. Supp. 748 (N.D. Miss. 1969).
10. The same court subsequently applied its decision in *Perry* to another school district: *Shull v. Columbus Municipal Separate School District*, 338 F. Supp. 1376 (N.D. Miss. 1972).
11. *Alvin Independent School District v. Cooper*, 404 S.W.2d 76 (Tex. Ct. of Civ. App. 1966).
12. *Wort v. Vierling*, 778 F.2d 1233 (7th Cir. 1985).
13. *Holt v. Shelton*, 341 F. Supp. 821 (M.D. Tenn. 1972).
14. *Davis v. Meek*, 344 F. Supp. 298 (N.D. Ohio 1972).
15. *Wellsand v. Valparaiso Community Schools Corporation*, Civil Action No. 71-H122(2) (N.D. Ind. 1971). See also *Indiana High School Athletic Assn. v. Raike*, 329 N.E.2d 66 (Ct. App. Ind. 1975).
16. *Moran v. School District No. 7, Yellowstone County*, 350 F. Supp. 1180 (D. Mont. 1972). See also *Hollon v. Mathis Independent School District*, 358 F. Supp. 1269 (S.D. Tex. 1973).
17. *Romans v. Crenshaw*, 354 F. Supp. 868 (S.D. Tex. 1972).
18. *Johnson v. Board of Education*, Civil Action No. 172-70, (D. N.J. 4/17/70).
19. Idaho Attorney General Opinion, 11/3/69.

20. *Matter of Murphy*, 11 Ed. Dept. Rep. 180 (New York State Commissioner of Education 1972).

21. *State v. Priest*, 210 La. 389, 27 So.2d 173 (1946); *In re Goodwin*, 214 La. 1062, 39 So.2d 731 (1949); *In re Rogers*, 234 N.Y.S.2d 172 (1962).

XI

School Records

Every school makes a record of each student's academic and personal progress from the time he or she enters kindergarten until he or she graduates, and often it keeps this "cumulative record" for many years afterward. The record may include, as was noted in one New York case, "progress reports, subject grades, intelligence quotients, tests, achievement scores, medical records, psychological and psychiatric reports, selective guidance notes and the evaluations of students by educators."[1] In short, your school keeps a great deal of personal information about you permanently on file.

The National Education Association's *Code of Student Rights and Responsibilities* states: "Records are kept to assist the school in offering appropriate educational experiences to the student. The interest of the student must supersede all other purposes to which records might be put."

In fact, the reverse is often the case. School officials frequently use a student's record against him or her as a threat ("If you do that again, it will go in your record and end up in your college recommendations") or as the basis for a suspension or other serious disciplinary action. Often the information contained in school records is little more than an expression of personal opinion of the student by teachers and other school personnel. Such remarks as "[student] spoke strangely to girls in class"; "never gives anyone benefit of doubt"; "Black militant"; "disrespectful while class was saluting flag"; and "is unkind to old people" have appeared in the permanent records of students in the New York City schools.

At least one court has recognized that student records are not supposed to be gossip sheets, and it ordered a high school principal to expunge from a student's record a notation that he had criticized the school and the principal on a radio program.[2] New Hampshire specifically bars schools from keeping records "which reflect the political activities or beliefs of students." It is also one of the few states that require cumulative records to be destroyed when they are no longer current.

The biggest problems that arise in connection with school

records involve the matter of who has access to them. On the one hand, many schools maintain that records are so confidential that students and their parents cannot see them; on the other, schools sometimes allow anyone else who claims to have a legitimate interest—such as a police officer, social worker, or potential employer—to see these same confidential records. The right to have petty personal comments expunged from your record doesn't mean much if you cannot find out they are there; and even without gossip, your record contains personal information that you probably would not want many people to see. Fortunately, not only have courts recognized the hazards inherent in school record-keeping, but federal legislation gives students right of access to their own records while limiting the public's right to see it.

Do students and their parents have a right to see the student's own school records?

Yes. In 1974, Congress passed an amendment to the Family Educational Rights and Privacy Act (known as the Buckley amendment) which guarantees the parents of students (and students themselves who are over 18 or attending a postsecondary school) the right to examine their children's student records, provided the school receives some sort of federal funding.[3] The law applies to virtually every public institution and many private ones. State and local laws in many areas have applied the Buckley amendment to all schools. The law assumes that both parents have the right to access unless a court order or a binding legal agreement such as a custody agreement provides otherwise.

Under the Buckley amendment, a student under 18 can see his or her records if the school decides on its own to give the student access or if the parent tells the school in writing to do so. There are a few restrictions on access that apply to students but not to parents. For example, parents, but not students, are given access to psychiatric and other noneducational treatment records in the sole possession of those providing treatment. Students who are at least 18, however, can designate a physician or other professional whom the school must permit to inspect these records. Students may see confidential letters of recommendation unless they have waived the right to see them. Even then, they may see them if they are being used for something other than the purpose for which the waiver was given.

The Buckley amendment provides that schools must respond to a request to view records "within a reasonable period of time." This period can never exceed 45 days, but many states and cities specify shorter periods and impose additional restrictions. In Massachusetts, for instance, schools must honor requests within two consecutive weekdays,[4] may charge a reasonable fee for the cost of copies made of documents, and may insist that school officials be present during an inspection of the original records. Some states—for example, Oregon—require schools to provide the services of a person qualified to interpret or explain behavioral records if they are being released.[5]

In New York City and Massachusetts, the school is required to notify parents every year of their right to see their child's records.[6]

Do parents and students have a right to see special education records?

Under P.L. 94-142, parents have the right to "inspect and review" any education records relating to the student if the records are collected, maintained, or used pursuant to P.L. 94-142.[7] Even medical or psychological records, under the Buckley amendment, should be available to parents if they are part of the student's evaluation or included in the student's school files. This is especially true if the records concern diagnosis, since even the Buckley amendment limits access to records concerning "treatment."

What can be done about improper or inaccurate entries in a student's record?

The best protection against the accumulation of irrelevant or inaccurate information in a student's file is for parents regularly to inspect their children's records. Part of the reason that school officials are able to keep records that are frequently based on little more than hearsay and rumor is their assumption that no parent or student will ever ask to see the records. If more parents demanded to see their children's records, school officials might be more careful in checking their facts.

Under the Buckley amendment, if, upon checking your records, you find that they contain material that you believe is inaccurate or unfair, you have a right to meet informally with school officials to ask them to change the records. If they refuse, you have a right to a formal hearing, to be held within a reasonable time before an impartial hearing officer, at which you must have a full opportunity to present your side of the story. The decision, in writing, must also be rendered within a reasonable time.

If the decision is not to amend the record, the parent or eligible student may still place a statement into the records explaining why the entry is unfair or inaccurate. This explanation must be included any time the contested portion of the record is released to anyone.

New York City and the states of Washington and Massachusetts have another safeguard plan: students are permitted to contest the accuracy of any entry in their records and, if still not satisfied, to add their own version of the incident, before or instead of a formal hearing. In New York City, parents must be notified promptly whenever a derogatory remark is placed in their child's record and have the right to appeal to have it expunged, before going to a formal hearing.

Even if an entry is proper, it may not be appropriate to keep it on a student's record forever. Many school districts have policies about periodically reviewing and destroying outdated or irrelevant information in students' temporary or guidance records. In New York City public high schools, this review is supposed to take place twice a year. In Massachusetts, parents are supposed to be notified before temporary records are destroyed, in case they want to see them first. Again, it is important to inspect records at least once a year to make sure they do not contain more than they should.

Does a student have the right to have school records kept confidential from outsiders?

Yes. The Buckley amendment also provides that educational institutions must obtain the written consent of a student's parents before it may release personally identifiable data to anyone other than a specified list of persons, such as school officials or teachers within the school who have a "legitimate educational interest" in the student's records. Records can also be sent to a school to which the student is transferring, but only after the parent has a chance to request a copy and challenge anything improper. Schools may turn over records in compliance with a lawful court order or subpoena only if they make a reasonable effort to notify the parent before they comply. They may turn over student records in an emergency only if the information disclosed is strictly necessary to protect the health or safety of the student or others. "Directory information" such as name, address, telephone number, or academic major can be released to the general public only if the school notifies parents each year as to what information will be released. The parent may request that the school not include the student on the list. A log must be kept as part of the student's records, indicating which third parties have requested or obtained information and why they were given access. Some states have additional protections. For instance, in Oregon, only a superintendent can release subpoenaed records. In Michigan, no record can be released without the parent's consent (or the student's, if the student is over eighteen).[8]

Some schools ask parents at the beginning of a school year, or at the time when their children first enter school, to sign a form which, among other things, gives the school the authority to release at its own discretion information from student records to inquiring outsiders. This kind of blanket authorization leads to many abuses. Parents may be happy to release certain information to a social worker but unwilling to release the same information to the police department. They may also change their minds about the release of their child's school record when certain new information is added. By requesting parents to sign a blanket authorization for release of information, the school is asking them to sign away rights concerning their child. Instead, parents should ask that their permission be obtained each time the school wishes to release information.

Finally, if a parent or a student over 18 tells the school in writing to release specified records to someone else such as a lawyer, relative, counselor, or friend, the school must comply.

At what age may students rather than their parents have access to and control over the release of their school records?

Under the Buckley amendment, the age is 18 or whenever a student starts to attend a postsecondary school. Different laws exist in some states. Delaware, for example, permits students from the age of 14 to control the release of their own records. In Massachusetts, once a student reaches age 14 or enters the ninth grade, the student has the same rights as his or her parents regarding school records. In New York City, high school students can see their permanent school records (e.g., grades, attendance, test scores) without parental permission, but they need parental permission to view their guidance records.

NOTES

1. *Matter of Thibadeau*, 1 Ed. Dept. Rep. 607 (New York State Commissioner of Education 1960).
2. *Matter of Shakin v. Schuker*, Index No. 6312/71 (Sup. Ct. Queens Co. 11/16/71).
3. P.L. 93-380, 20 U.S.C. §1232g. Regulations interpreting this law are found at 34 C.F.R. §§99 *et seq.*
4. Massachusetts Department of Education, *Regulations Pertaining to Student Records*, amended 1976.
5. Oreg. Rev. Stat. §336.195.
6. New York City Chancellor's Regulation A-820, 1979.
7. 34 C.F.R. §300.562.
8. Mich. Comp. Laws §600.2165.

XII

Grades and Diplomas

Can students be denied a diploma for misconduct if they have fulfilled all the academic requirements for graduation?

Although few legal precedents in this area have been established for public school students, a decision of the chancellor of the New York City schools, binding on all high schools in that city, is significant. The ruling came out of the following situation. The New York high school diploma included some mention of "citizenship" as well as of academic achievement. One principal, therefore, temporarily withheld the diploma of a student who, he felt, was not a "good citizen," even though the student had completed all his academic work for graduation. The chancellor, in holding that the diploma must be issued, wrote:

> Students who violate rules of conduct are subject to disciplinary measures, but the manipulation of a diploma is not a proper or legitimate disciplinary tool in view of the inherent difficulty in defining "citizenship" and the clear danger and impropriety of labelling students as "good" or "bad" citizens. The school system should award the diploma on the basis of carefully defined educational criteria, and not deny or delay the diploma on other than educational grounds or as a means of discipline. In brief, the school is empowered to grant diplomas, not citizenship.[1]

Can a student be denied a diploma for failing gym?

The law is unclear in most states. The New York State Commissioner of Education has ruled that "boards of education may not refuse graduation or promotion because of failure in physical education."[2] Students, therefore, must be granted diplomas even if they are not able to perform certain required exercises.

Failing to participate in a required gym class may be treated differently from inability to perform well in gym, although in a California case the court ordered the school to graduate a student who had been unable to graduate because he'd been given a failing grade in physical education for refusing to run laps around the gymnasium as punishment for being on the losing side of a volleyball game.[3]

Nevertheless, students run a clear risk in not attending gym class if gym is a required subject. If an attempt is made to keep you from graduating because you cut gym, you have several possible arguments. If you were not given advance notice of the consequences of cutting gym, then your due process rights were violated. If other students are exempted from gym or their absence is simply overlooked, then the rule is not being applied fairly and consistently, and denying you a diploma would be arbitrary and capricious.

Can school officials discipline students by barring them from graduation exercises?

Again, the answer is probably no. In a 1971 case in New York State, the court ruled that a school district could not bar a high school student who had satisfactorily completed her studies but who had allegedly struck and threatened her principal during a disturbance at the school. The court ruled there was no evidence that her presence at graduation ceremonies would be disruptive, so that barring her from participating would not be "a reasonable punishment meant to encourage the best educational results." It added: "It would indeed be a distortion of our educational process in this period of youthful discontent to snatch from a young woman at the point of educational fruition the savoring of her educational success."[4]

Similarly, the decision of a New York City junior high school to bar a student from graduation exercises was reversed by the New York State Commissioner of Education because the grounds for her punishment—"lack of good citizenship"—were too vague. In addition, the commissioner said: "It is educationally unsound for a school system to brand an individual with the label of 'poor citizen.' The placing of such a label upon a student is not a proper function of a school system."[5]

When a married, pregnant student was barred from graduation exercises because of her condition, the New York State Commissioner of Education again overruled the school district's decision.[6]

Is a student entitled to due process before being denied a diploma or being barred from attending graduation?

Students have a substantial interest in receiving a diploma and therefore it cannot be denied without due process. For instance, in one case in which the student was denied permission to take certain regents exams after being accused of cheating, and as a result did not receive a regents-endorsed diploma, the court found she was entitled to a hearing to determine whether she was in fact guilty of the charges.[7]

Some courts have found that students have a protected interest in participating in graduation ceremonies, and thus that due process is required before a student is barred.[8] But one court has said that while students have an interest in their diploma they do not have a protected interest in the graduation ceremony itself; therefore, it found no due process requirement.[9]

Can schools exclude students for poor academic performance?

Because there is no absolute right to go to private school or college or graduate school, these institutions are free to set academic standards for students' retention in school. Courts will not second-guess academic decisions unless those decisions are motivated by bad faith or ill will unrelated to academic performance or predicated on arbitrary and capricious factors not reasonably related to academic criteria.

In contrast, public high schools should not have the power to dismiss a student for poor academic performance since in virtually every state students are entitled to attend public school until they either earn a diploma or turn 21. Moreover, most states specify permissible grounds for suspension or expulsion in statute. If such statutes do not include academic failure as a ground, the school would be exceeding its authority if it excluded a student on that ground.

But high schools in Lexington, Kentucky, are doing just that. The school district's policy says that students over age 16 who do not earn a certain number of academic points are placed on academic probation the following school year. If they do not earn a set minimum of points during the quarters they are on probation, they "will be automatically dropped from school for the remainder of the school year." Ninety-nine students were dismissed from high school in one year alone under this policy. There is no provision for a hearing, and school district officials maintain that none is required since the dismissal is for academic rather than disciplinary reasons. The policy, currently under challenge in the state courts,[10] has been justly criticized. As one editorial in a local paper put it, "When it comes to young people with continuing academic woes, school officials find it easier to dismiss them with less consideration than would be given a student who, say, robbed a high school of its annual allotment of toilet paper. . . . The Fayette County schools should immediately and permanently consign the academic dismissal policy to the rubbish heap. It is far better to trash the policy than to continue to trash the students."[11]

Can a student's grade be lowered as punishment for absences?

School policies vary widely from state to state. In New York State, the education commissioner has ruled that cutting class and truancy are behavioral, not academic, offenses. While students can receive disciplinary sanctions for unexcused absences, they should not receive automatic grade reductions or failures. If class participation is part of the grade, that policy should be announced at the beginning of the term, and absent students should have an opportunity to make up for missed work regardless of whether their absence was excused or not.[12]

The New Jersey State Commissioner of Education takes a slightly different tack, forbidding the lowering of grades but permitting school boards to set attendance policies that deny students credit altogether. The rationale is that the averaging in of a low or failing grade will have a permanent punitive effect on the student's record, while simply denying credit allows the student to make up the class by starting over fresh. Students must be given adequate notice of such attendance policies; then, if necessary, an opportunity for a hearing; and, if the absence is legitimate, a chance to make up missed work. If a student is prone to cutting or truancy, he or she must have counseling.[13]

In some states, school districts have been found to be exceeding their authority in setting policies providing for automatic grade reductions or loss of credit after a certain number of absences because such rules are not included in or permitted by state statutes dealing with truancy.[14]

In one case, a student challenged a college policy that students who miss four classes "may" be removed from the program. The court ruled that the decision was arbitrary because the school did not attempt to evaluate the effect of absences and should have given the student a chance to show that he had learned the material covered in his absence.[15]

In another case, a school reduced a student's grade in several courses after she left school on an emergency without advising the school staff as was required by the school policy on unexcused absences. The court said the school had to show that the grade reduction penalty in this girl's case was reasonably related to the disciplinary objectives of the school board's policy on unexcused absences.[16]

Can students be penalized for work missed because of a suspension?

Many school districts and some states have laws or rules requiring schools to permit suspended students to make up work and take final exams. A Kentucky court ruled that a school which said in its handbook that suspended students were subject to grade reductions for days missed and could not make up missed work exceeded its authority in imposing this extra penalty because the state law on suspensions did not provide for academic penalties.[17] The New York State Commissioner of Education has ruled that school boards "may not subvert the purpose of grading by arbitrarily reducing a student's grades as a means of imposing discipline."[18] The New Jersey State Commissioner of Education forbids schools from counting student absences during suspensions to determine breaches by students of attendance policy because that would constitute a forbidden double penalty. A suspended student must be given the opportunity to make up any work missed and must be graded as if the work were received on time.[19]

NOTES

1. *Matter of Carroll*, Decision of New York City Chancellor (12/6/71).
2. *Matter of O'Brien*, 13 Ed. Dept. Rep. 276 (1974); *Matter of Rafferty*, 11 Ed. Dept. Rep. 53 (1971); *Matter of Walsh*, 10 Ed. Dept. Rep. 36 (1970); *Matter of Cohen*, 1 Ed. Dept. Rep. 689 (1961).
3. *Coats v. Cloverdale Unified School District Governing Board*, Civil

Action No. 80029 (Calif. Sup. Ct. Sonoma Cty. 1/2/75) (Clearinghouse No. 1 14,462).

4. *Ladson v. Board of Education, Union Free School District No. 9,* 323 N.Y.S.2d 545 (S. Ct. Nassau Co. 1971).

5. *Matter of Wilson,* 11 Ed. Dept. Rep. 208 (1972).

6. *Matter of Murphy,* 11 Ed. Dept. Rep. 180 (1972).

7. *Goldwyn v. Allen,* 281 N.Y.S.2d 899 (S. Ct. Queens Co. 1967).

8. *Clark v. Board of Education,* 367 N.E.2d 69 (Ohio Common Pleas 1977); *Castillo v. South Conejos School District,* RE-10, Civil Action No. 79-CV, (Colo. Dist. Ct. Conejos Cty. 4/18/79).

9. *Fowler v. Williamson,* 448 F. Supp. 497 (W.D. N.C. 1978).

10. *Simons v. Fayette County Board of Education,* Civil Action No. 86-CI-775 (Fayette Cir. Ct., Civil Branch, 3d Div., preliminary injunction denied, 4/16/86).

11. "Academic Dismissal Policy Is a Candidate for Expulsion," *Lexington Herald-Leader,* April 22, 1986, p. A8.

12. *Matter of Caskey,* 21 Ed. Dept. Rep. 138 (1981); *Matter of Moller,* 21 Ed. Dept. Rep. 188 (1981).

13. *Wetherell v. Board of Education of Burlington Township,* 1978 S.L.D. 20; *Wheatley v. Board of Education of Burlington,* 1974 S.L.D. 851; *C.G. v. Board of Education of David Brearly High School,* 1980 S.L.D. 1178.

14. *Opinion of the Attorney General,* No. CV 74-145 (Calif. 8/13/75); *Gutierrez v. School District R-1, Otero City,* 585 P.2d 935 (Colo. App. Ct. 1978). But cf. *Knight v. Board of Education of Tri-Point Community Unity School Dist.,* 348 N.E.2d 299 (Ill. App. 1976).

15. *Kelley v. Charles Steward Mott Community College,* Civil Action No. 80-40397 (E.D. Mich. 2/9/81).

16. *Hamer v. Board of Education of Township High School District No. 113, County Lake,* 383 N.E.2d 231 (Ill. App. 1978).

17. *Dorsey v. Bale,* 521 S.W.2d 76 (Ky. App. 1975).

18. *Matter of MacWhinnie,* 20 Ed. Dept. Rep. 145 (1980).

19. *Haddad v. Cranford Board of Education,* 1968 S.L.D. 98.

XIII

Private Schools

The discussion of student rights in this book is mainly applicable to public school students. That is not to say, however, that private and parochial school students have no rights.

Can private and parochial schools discriminate on the basis of race or national origin?

The Supreme Court has ruled that private, nonsectarian schools are prohibited from discriminating on the basis of race by the Civil Rights Act of 1866, commonly referred to as Section 1981.[1] This act was passed by Congress to eradicate the "badges of slavery" after the Thirteenth Amendment abolished slavery. The Supreme Court has not decided whether parochial schools are prohibited from practicing racial discrimination that is based on religious doctrine, although it has been said such schools may be denied tax-exempt status if they discriminate.[2] Lower federal courts, in upholding the illegality of excluding blacks from admission and expelling white students for interracial dating, have concluded that the religious schools acted from political or social beliefs, not religious principles, so that the free exercise of religion clause of the First Amendment was not violated.[3] But religious grounds still do not justify discrimination, according to one panel of judges that heard a racial exclusion case. While they saw a school's exclusionary policies as based on religious belief, they said the need to eradicate the badges of slavery outweighed the right to free exercise of religion.[4]

The federal circuit courts are divided on whether discrimination on the basis of national origin is also prohibited by Section 1981. However, discrimination on the basis of race, color or national origin is prohibited in any school program or activity that receives federal funds, under Title VI of the Civil Rights Act of 1964.

Can private and parochial schools discriminate on the basis of gender or handicap?

While Section 1981 does not apply to discrimination on the

basis of gender or handicap, such discrimination is prohibited for any program or activity receiving federal funds. Section 504 of the Rehabilitation Act of 1973[5] forbids exclusion, discrimination, or denial of benefits on the basis of handicap, while Title IX of the Education Amendments of 1972[6] contains the same prohibitions on discrimination based on gender. The Supreme Court has interpreted these statutes to cover only the specific activity or program that receives federal funding, not the school as a whole. Congress is considering amending these statutes so that a private or parochial school may not discriminate in any way if it receives federal funds for any purpose.

Handicapped students placed in private schools by a public agency at public expense are guaranteed the same rights as handicapped students in public schools through the Education for All Handicapped Children Act (P.L. 94-142). Handicapped children who attend private schools but were not placed there by public agencies are still entitled to publicly funded special education services if they need them.

Do students in nonpublic schools have due process rights?

Private and parochial school students may have due process rights, but not necessarily for the same reasons or to the same extent as public school students. The Fourteenth Amendment applies to "state action," that is, action by an official or an agency of state or local government. Courts look for state action in a private school on a case-by-case basis. They ask whether the school as a whole is under the control of or acting on behalf of the government, and they inquire whether a government agency shares responsibility for the specific act or activity that is being challenged, through government regulation, financial aid, etc.

The courts usually conclude there is no state action.[7] The constitutional right to due process probably ordinarily applies if the specific actions in question by the nonpublic school are funded, regulated, or approved of by some public agency, or if the student who is adversely affected was placed in the school by a public agency.

A private school student may have a contractual right to due process. School catalogs and handbooks are considered by courts to be part of the contract between the buyer of educational services (the student) and the seller (the school). If the literature says that a hearing will be held before a student is expelled, then the student has a contractual right to such a hearing. In one case where the university specifically provided for a hearing before expulsion of a student, the court said it would review the procedures to make sure they met the "reasonable expectations" of a student reading the relevant university rules and would examine the hearing to make sure it had been conducted fairly. But the same court said that it would not question the school's decision to expel or suspend a student if there was no stated policy providing for a hearing.[8] In another case, the court held that students had no right to notice or a hearing before an expulsion because, according to the catalog, the school reserved the right to expel without mentioning a hearing.[9]

A different line of cases says that private institutions must have fair procedures not because of any contractual agreement, but because students have interests in their degrees and in their reputations that the courts should protect. These cases balance student interests against the importance of the private school's integrity and independence. In one such case, where a student was suspended for one year for allegedly violating Princeton University's honor code, the court concluded, "Princeton must have established procedures for safeguarding that [the student's] interest, and, if it strays from its own rules, Princeton must have good and sufficient reasons for doing so."[10] In another case, the court said that Princeton could not have someone arrested for criminal trespass for selling political materials on its campus because the university did not have a reasonable regulatory scheme designed to protect both its legitimate interests as an institution of higher education and the individual exercise of freedom of expression.[11] In a third case, a New York court ruled that "a private university cannot expel, bar and fine a student without following fair and reasonable procedures. It cannot be arbitrary. It must abide by constitutional principles of fair conduct implicit in our society."[12]

Private schools probably have more discretion to expel a student for poor academic performance than for disciplinary reasons. Courts do not want to second-guess schools on academic standards and will overturn such expulsions only if the school has acted in an arbitrary and capricious fashion. In one

case a court did order a school to readmit a student because
an appeals committee had allowed other students who had
failed the same number of courses to repeat the year's work.
The court found that the school's failure to apply its procedures
and standards equally to all students was arbitrary and capricious and an abuse of discretion.[13] But in a different sort of
case, a student leader with an otherwise blameless record was
accused of plagiarism after failing to attribute the source of a
quote on a Spanish term paper. Here the court upheld the
university's decision to withhold the student's bachelor's degree for a year, saying that it would not "engraft its own views"
on a private school's student disciplinary process, so long as
that process met the "standard of good faith and fair-dealing."[14]

Do private school students have rights in regard to their school records?

The Family Educational Rights and Privacy Act (FERPA;
often referred to as the Buckley amendment), which protects
the privacy of student records and requires schools to show
records on request to parents or adult students,[15] applies only
to nonpublic schools that receive federal funds. Few private
schools below the college level receive federal funds. Some
states and cities, however, have applied the Buckley amendment to all schools through statute or regulation. Others have
open-record laws applying to any school that receives state
funds.

Sometimes schools try to withhold student transcripts because of unpaid tuition. A Texas attorney general said that one
such school could lose its accreditation if it did not allow parents
to "inspect and review" student records, because the school
participated in a federal school lunch program and was therefore
covered by FERPA. A California attorney general ruled that
under state law both public and private schools are obligated
to transfer records upon the request of the school to which a
student has transferred because withholding records might mean
the student couldn't attend school. This would be prohibited
under the law of the state.[16] Similarly, a New York court ordered
a private school to honor a parent's request that a transcript
be sent to the student's new school even though tuition was
owed.[17]

NOTES

1. *Runyon v. McCrary*, 427 U.S. 160 (1960); 42 U.S.C. §1981.

2. *Bob Jones University v. U.S.*, 461 U.S. 574 (1983).

3. *Fiedler v. Marumsco Christian School*, 631 F.2d 1144 (4th Cir. 1980).

4. *Brown v. Dade Christian Schools*, 556 F.2d 310 (5th Cir. 1977), *en banc cert. denied*, 98 S. Ct. 1235 (1978).

5. Title VI of the Civil Rights Act of 1964, 20 U.S.C. §2000d, 34 C.F.R. §100.3(b); Title IX of the 1972 Educational Amendments, 20 U.S.C. §1681, 34 C.F.R. Part 106; §504 of the Rehabilitation Act of 1973, 29 U.S.C. §794, C.F.R. Part 104.

6. *Grove City College v. Bell*, 465 U.S. 555 (1984).

7. State action found: *Albert v. Carovano*, No. 87–7111; (2d Cir. 1987). *Milonas v. Williams*, 691 F.2d 931 (10th Cir. 1982), *cert. denied*, 460 U.S. 1069 (1983); *Isaacs v. Board of Trustees of Temple University*, 385 F. Supp. 473 (E.D. Pa. 1974); *Ryan v. Hofstra University*, 324 N.Y.S.2d 964 (Sup. Ct. Nassau Cty. 1971); *Coleman v. Wagner College*, 420 F.2d 1120 (2d Cir. 1970). State action not found: *Rendell-Baker v. Kohn*, 457 U.S. 830 (1982); *Williams v. Howard University*, 528 F.2d 658 (D.C. Cir. 1976), *cert. denied*, 429 U.S. 850 (1977); *Rice v. Presidents and Fellows of Harvard University*, 663 F.2d 336 (1st Cir. 1981); *Sament v. Hahnemann Medical College*, 413 F. Supp. 434 (E.D. Pa. 1976), *aff'd*, 547 F.2d 1164 (3d Cir. 1977); *Powe v. Miles*, 407 F.2d 73 (2d Cir. 1968).

8. *Cloud v. Trustees of Boston University*, 720 F.2d 721, 724 (1st Cir. 1983).

9. *Greene v. Howard University*, 271 F. Supp. 609, 614 (D. D.C. 1967); remanded 412 F.2d 609.

10. *Clayton v. Trustees of Princeton University*, 519 F. Supp. 802 (D. N.J. 1981); 608 F. Supp. 413 (D. N.J. 1985). See also *Rutledge v. Guilian*, 93 N.J. 113 (Sup. Ct. 1983).

11. *State v. Schmid*, 84 N.J. 535 (Sup. Ct. 1980).

12. *Ryan v. Hofstra University*, *supra*.

13. *Heister v. Albany Medical College*, 453 N.Y.S. 2d 196 (N.Y. Sup. Ct. 1982).

14. *Harris v. Trustees of Columbia University* 468 N.E.2d 54 (N.Y. A.D. 1st Dept. 1983).

15. 20 U.S.C. §1232g; 34 C.F.R. Part 99.

16. 64 Ops. Calif. Atty. Gen. 867, No. 81-511, 12/11/81. See also Oreg. Laws §336.215(2) which flatly requires private schools to release records.

17. *Sargent v. St. Paul's School for Boys*, *New York Law Journal*, 4/15/80, p. 11, col. 4.

Afterword

The preceding chapters have tried to describe what legal rights students have in a public school. By this point it may have occurred to you that students at your school, in fact, have few of these rights. Can you do anything about it? As we mentioned at the outset, there are not enough lawyers available to bring lawsuits to secure every right of every student. So just as a practical matter, you may well have to consider other means for securing them. Sometimes, in fact, it is preferable to use other means whether or not lawyers are available. Lawsuits can take months to resolve and, of course, may finally be lost, leaving the school policy unchanged. Many students, moreover, believe that broader and more permanent change in school policy results when students are involved in bringing about change than when a court declares a specific practice illegal.

There is, finally, perhaps a more important reason why lawyers should not be relied on too extensively. Although lawyers can be helpful in dealing with the range of problems discussed in this book, students remain unfree in a variety of other ways, big and small, which are part of the accepted routine at most schools and which no lawyer will be able to challenge through the courts.

Underlying this unfree condition is "the assumption that the state has the right to compel adolescents to spend six or seven hours a day, five days a week, 36 or so weeks a year, in a specific place, under the charge of a particular group of persons in whose selection they have no voice, performing tasks about which they have no choice, without remuneration, and subject to specialized regulations and sanctions that are applicable to no one else in the community nor to them except in this place."[1] That is an assumption that no court has yet directly challenged. Indirectly, yes, by declaring that students do have some rights. But for even those rights to be most meaningful, they must be directed toward establishing the proposition that students "have the right to influence the effects the institution has on them. As other institutions exist to serve their clients, schools at all levels exist so that people attending them can learn. More than most institutions, schools influence the course of their clients' present and future lives. Students therefore have the right to substantial influence over the educational program, including the goals they pursue, the topics they study, the learning materials and learning processes they use, and the criteria for evaluating accomplishments."[2]

A variety of means are available to students to secure a greater degree of participation in running their schools. It is beyond the scope of this book to suggest the most effective means in your school, although some of the references in the bibliography may give you useful suggestions.

NOTES

1. Edgar Z. Friedenberg, *Coming of Age in America* (1965).
2. *Code of Student Rights and Responsibilities*, National Education Association (1971).

Appendix A

How to Use This Book

At the end of each chapter, notes give references to the decisions of various courts; to the decisions of school officials; to statutes in state law; to the policy of a board of education or a state department of education. These citations will be of use mostly to lawyers, but you may decide to show the actual decision, law, or policy to a school official. A word, then, about how to find the reference.

1. Most court decisions are referred to, or "cited," by the series of volumes in which they appear. For example, the citation for *Tinker v. Des Moines Independent Community School District* is 393 U.S. 503 (1969). This means that the case appears in volume 393 of the series called *United States Reports*, beginning on page 503; the case was decided in 1969. Similarly, "F.2d" or "F. Supp." in a citation refers to another series of volumes in which cases can be found. Again, the numbers refer to the particular volume and page where the decision is printed. The series of volumes containing the decisions can be found in a law library or courthouse in most cities, and a lawyer or law librarian should be able to point you toward the right shelves.

A few court decisions are cited differently, such as *Caldwell v. Cannady*, Civil Action No. CA-5-994 (N.D. Tex. 1/27/72). Such decisions have not been printed (at least as of the time that this book was published) and can be obtained by writing the clerk of the court that decided the case (copying costs will generally be charged). The number and date after the name of the case will enable you to identify the case precisely. A lawyer can tell you where to write.

2. Decisions of a commissioner of education can usually be obtained by writing to the commissioner at the department of education in the state capital. Again, the number after the name of the case helps to identify it.

Decisions of the Chancellor or Board of Education of New

York City can be obtained by writing to Secretary, Board of
Education, 110 Livingston Street, Brooklyn, New York 11201.

3. Citations to state laws such as N.H. Rev. State Ann., Title
VI, generally refer to volumes available in a law library and
sometimes in a lawyer's office.

Policies of a state department of education should be available
from the department in the state capital.

Your school *must* obey the following: federal statutes and
regulations; decisions of the U.S. Supreme Court; decisions of
other federal courts in your area; decisions of the state courts
in your area, especially your state's highest court; your state's
statutes and regulations; your state education department's
decisions, policies, and rules; and the decisions, rules, and
policies of your school board or district. A lawyer can easily
tell you whether a course of law cited in this book is legally
binding on your school. If it is not, it can still be used as a
model for what the policy should be in your school. Your task
would be to explain the legal or educational reasons why the
policy is mandated somewhere and why it is equally appropriate
for your school.

Once you know what your arguments are, how do you get
to make them?

You can find out the rules for formally appealing school
actions by checking your student handbook or contacting your
school district or school board office. In the case of suspensions
and expulsions, there are almost certainly procedures for appealing decisions, and you should follow them to the letter.
But if you are part of a group that wishes to change a general
school policy, informal negotiations with school authorities may
be an appropriate way to start.

Your local ACLU office may be able to advise you or put
you in touch with lawyers or citizens groups that provide advocacy for students. There are also two national organizations
that you can write to for information about groups in your area.
They are:

The National Coalition of Advocates for Students
100 Boylston Street, Suite 737
Boston, Massachusetts 02116

The National Committee for Citizens in Education
10840 Little Patuxent Parkway, Suite 301
Columbia, Maryland 21044

   Toll free number for information: 1-800--638-9675
   Monday–Friday, 10 A.M.–4 P.M. Eastern Time

Appendix B

Tinker v. Des Moines Independent Community School District, 393 U.S. 503 (1969)

MR. JUSTICE FORTAS delivered the opinion of the Court.

Petitioner John F. Tinker, 15 years old, and petitioner Christopher Eckhardt, 16 years old, attended high schools in Des Moines. Petitioner Mary Beth Tinker, John's sister, was a 13-year-old student in junior high school.

In December 1965 a group of adults and students in Des Moines, Iowa, held a meeting at the Eckhardt home. The group determined to publicize their objections to the hostilities in Vietnam and their support for a truce by wearing black armbands during the holiday season and by fasting on December 16 and New Year's Eve. Petitioners and their parents had previously engaged in similar activities, and they decided to participate in the program.

The principals of the Des Moines schools became aware of the plan to wear armbands. On December 14, 1965, they met and adopted a policy that any student wearing an armband to school would be asked to remove it, and if he refused he would be suspended until he returned without the armband. Petitioners were aware of the regulation that the school authorities adopted.

On December 16, Mary Beth and Christopher wore black armbands to their schools. John Tinker wore his armband the next day. They were all sent home and suspended from school until they would come back without their armbands. They did not return to school until after the planned period for wearing armbands had expired—that is, until after New Year's Day.

This complaint was filed in the United States District Court by petitioners, through their fathers, under § 1983 of Title 42 of the United States Code. It prayed for an injunction restraining the defendant school officials and the defendant members of the board of directors of the school district from disciplining the petitioners, and it sought nominal damages. After an evidentiary hearing the District Court dismissed the complaint. It upheld the constitutionality of the school authorities' action on the ground that it was reasonable in order to prevent disturbance of school discipline. 258 F. Supp. 971 (1966). The court referred to but expressly declined to follow the Fifth Circuit's holding in a similar case that prohibition of the wearing of symbols like the armbands cannot be sustained unless it "materially and substantially interfere[s] with the requirements of appropriate discipline in the operation of the school." *Burnside v. Byars*, 363 F.2d 744, 749 (1966).[1]

On appeal, the Court of Appeals for the Eighth Circuit considered the case *en banc*. The court was equally divided, and the District Court's decision was accordingly affirmed, without opinion. 383 F.2d 988 (1967). We granted certiorari. 390 U.S. (1968).

I

The District Court recognized that the wearing of an armband for the purpose of expressing certain views is the type of symbolic act that is within the Free Speech Clause of the First Amendment. See *West Virginia v. Barnette*, 319 U.S. 624 (1943); *Stromberg v. California*, 283 U.S. 359 (1931). Cf. *Thornhill v. Alabama*, 310 U.S. 88 (1940); *Edwards v. South Carolina*, 372 U.S. 229 (1963); *Brown v. Louisiana*, 383 U.S. 131 (1966). As we shall discuss, the wearing of armbands in the circumstances of this case was entirely divorced from actually or potentially disruptive conduct by those participating in it. It was closely akin to "pure speech" which, we have repeatedly held, is entitled to comprehensive protection under the First Amendment. Compare *Cox v. Louisiana*, 379 U.S. 536, 555 (1965); *Adderley v. Florida*, 385 U.S. 39 (1966).

First Amendment rights, applied in light of the special characteristics of the school environment, are available to teachers and students. It can hardly be argued that either students or teachers shed their constitutional rights to freedom of speech

or expression at the schoolhouse gate. This has been the un-
mistakable holding of this Court for almost 50 years. In *Meyer
v. Nebraska*, 262 U.S. 390 (1923), and *Bartels v. Iowa*, 262
U.S. 404 (1923), this Court, in opinions by Mr. Justice
McReynolds, held that the Due Process Clause of the Fourteenth Amendment prevents States from forbidding the teaching of a foreign language to young students. Statutes to this
effect, the Court held, unconstitutionally interfere with the
liberty of teacher, student, and parent.[2] See also *Pierce v.
Society of Sisters*, 268 U.S. 510 (1925); *West Virginia v. Barnette*, 319 U.S. 624 (1943); *McCollum v. Board of Education*,
333 U.S. 203 (1948); *Wieman v. Updegraff*, 344 U.S. 183, 195
(1952) (concurring opinion); *Sweezy v. New Hampshire*, 354
U.S. 234 (1957); *Shelton v. Tucker*, 364 U.S. 479, 487 (1960);
Engel v. Vitale, 370 U.S. 421 (1962); *Keyishian v. Board of
Regents*, 385 U.S. 589, 603 (1967); *Epperson v. Arkansas*, 393
U.S. 97 (1968).

In *West Virginia v. Barnette*, *supra*, this Court held that
under the First Amendment, the student in public school may
not be compelled to salute the flag. Speaking through Mr.
Justice Jackson, the Court said:

> The Fourteenth Amendment, as now applied to the States,
> protects the citizen against the State itself and all of its
> creatures—Boards of Education not excepted. These have,
> of course, important, delicate, and highly discretionary
> functions, but none that they may not perform within the
> limits of the Bill of Rights. That they are educating the
> young for citizenship is reason for scrupulous protection
> of Constitutional freedoms of the individual, if we are not
> to strangle the free mind at its source and teach youth to
> discount important principles of our government as mere
> platitudes. 319 U.S., at 637.

On the other hand, the Court has repeatedly emphasized
the need for affirming the comprehensive authority of the States
and of school authorities, consistent with fundamental constitutional safeguards, to prescribe and control conduct in the
schools. See *Epperson v. Arkansas*, *supra*, at 194; *Meyer v.
Nebraska*, *supra*, at 402. Our program lies in the area where
students in the exercise of First Amendment rights collide with
the rules of the school authorities.

II

The problem presented by the present case does not relate to regulation of the length of skirts or the type of clothing, to hair style or deportment. Compare *Ferrell v. Dallas Independent School District*, 392 F.2d 697 (1968); *Pugsley v. Sellmeyer*, 158 Ark. 247, 250 S.W. 538 (1923). It does not concern aggressive, disruptive action or even group demonstrations. Our problem involves direct, primary First Amendment rights akin to "pure speech."

The school officials banned and sought to punish petitioners for a silent, passive expression of opinion, unaccompanied by any disorder or disturbance on the part of petitioners. There is here no evidence whatever of petitioners' interference, actual or nascent, with the school's work or of collision with the rights of other students to be secure and to be let alone. Accordingly, this case does not concern speech or action that intrudes upon the work of the school or the rights of other students.

Only a few of the 18,000 students in the school system wore the black armbands. Only five students were suspended for wearing them. There is no indication that the work of the school or any class was disrupted. Outside the classrooms, a few students made hostile remarks to the children wearing armbands, but there were no threats or acts of violence on school premises.

The District Court concluded that the action of the school authorities was reasonable because it was based upon their fear of a disturbance from the wearing of the armbands. But, in our system, undifferentiated fear or apprehension of disturbance is not enough to overcome the right to freedom of expression. Any departure from absolute regimentation may cause trouble. Any variation from the majority's opinion may inspire fear. Any word spoken, in class, in the lunchroom, or on the campus, that deviates from the views of another person, may start an argument or cause a disturbance. But our Constitution says we must take this risk. *Terminiello v. Chicago*, 337 U.S. 1. (1959); and our history says that it is this sort of hazardous freedom—this kind of openness—that is the basis of our National strength and of the independence and vigor of Americans who grow up and live in this relatively permissive, often disputatious society.

In order for the State in the person of school officials to justify prohibition of a particular expression of opinion, it must be able to show that its action was caused by something more than a mere desire to avoid the discomfort and unpleasantness that always accompany an unpopular viewpoint. Certainly where there is no finding and no showing that the exercise of the forbidden right would "materially and substantially interfere with the requirements of appropriate discipline in the operation of the school," the prohibition cannot be sustained. *Burnside v. Byars, supra,* at 749.

In the present case, the District Court made no such finding, and our independent examination of the record fails to yield evidence that the school authorities had reason to anticipate that the wearing of the armbands would substantially interfere with the work of the school or impinge upon the rights of other students. Even an official memorandum prepared after the suspension that listed the reasons for the ban on wearing the armbands made no reference to the anticipation of such disruptions.[3]

On the contrary, the action of the school authorities appears to have been based upon an urgent wish to avoid the controversy which might result from the expression, even by the silent symbol of armbands, of opposition to this Nation's part in the conflagration in Vietnam.[4] It is revealing, in this respect, that the meeting at which the school principals decided to issue the contested regulation was called in response to a student's statement to the journalism teacher in one of the schools that he wanted to write an article on Vietnam and have it published in the school paper. (The student was dissuaded.)[5]

It is also relevant that the school authorities did not purport to prohibit the wearing of all symbols of political or controversial significance. The record shows that students in some of the schools wore buttons relating to national political campaigns, and some even wore the Iron Cross, traditionally a symbol of nazism. The order prohibiting the wearing of armbands did not extend to these. Instead, a particular symbol—black armbands worn to exhibit opposition to this Nation's involvement in Vietnam—was singled out for prohibition. Clearly, the prohibition of expression of one particular opinion, at least without evidence that it is necessary to avoid material and substantial interference with school work or discipline, is not constitutionally permissible.

In our system, state-operated schools may not be enclaves of totalitarianism. School officials do not possess absolute authority over their students. Students in school as well as out of school are "persons" under our Constitution. They are possessed of fundamental rights which the State must respect, just as they themselves must respect their obligations to the State. In our system, students may not be regarded as closed-circuit recipients of only that which the State chooses to communicate. They may not be confined to the expression of those sentiments that are officially approved. In the absence of a specific showing of constitutionally valid reasons to regulate their speech, students are entitled to freedom of expression of their views. As Judge Gewin, speaking for the Fifth Circuit, said, school officials cannot suppress "expressions of feelings with which they do not wish to contend." *Burnside v. Byars, supra*, at 749.

In *Meyer v. Nebraska, supra*, at 402, Justice McReynolds expressed this Nation's repudiation of the principle that a State might so conduct its schools as to "foster a homogeneous people." He said:

In order to submerge the individual and develop ideal citizens, Sparta assembled the males at seven into barracks and intrusted their subsequent education and training to official guardians. Although such measures have been deliberately approved by men of great genius, their ideas touching the relation between individual and State were wholly different from those upon which our institutions rest; and it hardly will be affirmed that any legislature could impose such restrictions upon the people of a State without doing violence to both letter and spirit of the Constitution.

This principle has been repeated by this Court on numerous occasions during the intervening years. In *Keyishian v. Board of Regents*, 385 U.S. 589, 603, MR. JUSTICE BRENNAN, speaking for the Court, said:

The vigilant protection of constitutional freedom is nowhere more vital than in the community of American schools.' *Shelton v. Tucker*, 234 U.S. 479, 487. The classroom is peculiarly the 'market-place of ideas.' The Nation's future depends upon leaders training through wide exposure to that robust exchange of ideas which discovers truth, out of a multitude of tongues, [rather] than through any kind of authoritative selection. . . .

The principle of these cases is not confined to the supervised and ordained discussion which takes place in the classroom. The principal use to which the schools are dedicated is to accommodate students during prescribed hours for the purpose of certain types of activities. Among those activities is personal intercommunication among the students.[6] This is not only an inevitable part of the process of attending school. It is also an important part of the educational process. A student's rights, therefore, do not embrace merely the classroom hours. When he is in the cafeteria, or on the playing field, or on the campus during the authorized hours, he may express his opinions, even on controversial subjects like the conflict in Vietnam, if he does so "without materially and substantially interfering with appropriate discipline in the operation of the school" and without colliding with the rights of others. *Burnside v. Byars, supra*, at 749. But conduct by the student, in class or out of it, which for any reason—whether it stems from time, place, or type of behavior—materially disrupts classwork or involves substantial disorder or invasion of the rights of others is, of course, not immunized by the constitutional guaranty of freedom of speech. Cf. *Blackwell v. Issaquena City Bd. of Educ.*, 303 F.2d 749 (C.A. 5th Cir. 1966).

Under our Constitution, free speech is not a right that is given only to be so circumscribed that it exists in principle but not in fact. Freedom of expression would not truly exist if the right could be exercised only in an area that a benevolent government has provided as a safe haven for crackpots. The Constitution says that Congress (and the States) may not abridge the right to free speech. This provision means what it says. We properly read it to permit reasonable regulation of speech-connected activities in carefully restricted circumstances. But we do not confine the permissible exercise of First Amendment rights to a telephone booth or the four corners of a pamphlet, or to supervised and ordained discussion in a school classroom.

If a regulation were adopted by school officials forbidding discussion of the Vietnam conflict, or the expression by any student of opposition to it anywhere on school property except as part of a prescribed classroom exercise, it would be obvious that the regulation would violate the constitutional rights of students, at least if it could not be justified by a showing that the student's activities would materially and substantially disrupt the work and discipline of the school. Cf. *Hammond v. South Carolina State College*, 272 F. Supp. 947 (D.C.D.S.C. 1967) (orderly protest meeting on state college campus); *Dickey v. Alabama State Board*, 273 F. Supp. 613 (D.C.M.D. Ala. 1967) (expulsion of student editor of college newspaper). In the circumstances of the present case, the prohibition of the silent, passive "witness of the armbands," as one of the children called it, is no less offensive to the Constitution's guaranties.

As we have discussed, the record does not demonstrate any facts which might reasonably have led school authorities to forecast substantial disruption of or material interference with school activities, and no disturbances or disorders on the school premises in fact occurred. These petitioners merely went about their ordained rounds in school. Their deviation consisted only in wearing on their sleeve a band of black cloth, not more than two inches wide. They wore it to exhibit their disapproval of the Vietnam hostilities and their advocacy of a truce, to make their views known, and by their example, to influence others to adopt them. They neither interrupted school activities nor sought to intrude in the school affairs or the lives of others. They caused discussion outside of the classrooms, but no interference with work and no disorder. In the circumstances, our Constitution does not permit officials of the State to deny their form of expression.

We express no opinion as to the form of relief which should be granted, this being a matter for the lower courts to determine. We reverse and remand for further proceedings consistent with this opinion.

Reversed and remanded.

NOTES

1. In *Burnside*, the Fifth Circuit ordered that high school authorities be enjoined from enforcing a regulation forbidding students to wear "freedom buttons." It is instructive that in *Blackwell v. Issaquena County Board of Education*, 363 F.2d 749 (1966), the same panel

on the same day reached the opposite result on different facts. It declined to enjoin enforcement of such a regulation in another high school where the students wearing freedom buttons harassed students who did not wear them and created much disturbance.

2. *Hamilton v. Regents of Univ. of Cal.*, 293 U.S. 245 (1934) is sometimes cited for the broad proposition that the State may attach conditions to attendance at a state university that require individuals to violate their religious convictions. The case involved dismissal of members of a religious denomination from a land grant college for refusal to participate in military training. Narrowly viewed, the case turns upon the Court's conclusion that merely requiring a student to participate in school training in military "science" could not conflict with his constitutionally protected freedom of conscience. The decision cannot be taken as establishing that the State may impose and enforce any conditions that it chooses upon attendance at public institutions of learning, however violative they may be of fundamental constitutional guaranties. See, e.g., *West Virginia v. Barnette*, 319 U.S. 624 (1943); *Dixon v. Alabama State Bd. of Educ.*, 294 F.2d 150 (C.A. 5th Cir. 1961); *Knight v. State Bd. of Educ.*, 200 F. Supp. 174 (D.C.M.D. Tenn. 1961); *Dickey v. Alabama St. Bd. of Educ.*, 273 F. Supp. 613 (C.A.M.D. Ala. 1967). See also Note, 73 Harv. L. Rev. 1595 (1960); Note, 81 Harv. L. Rev. 1045 (1968).

3. The only suggestions of fear of disorder in the report are these: "A former student of one of our high schools was killed in Vietnam. Some of his friends are still in school and it was felt that if any kind of a demonstration existed, it might evolve into something which would be difficult to control."

"Students at one of the high schools were heard to say they would wear arm bands of other colors if the black bands prevailed."

Moreover, the testimony of school authorities at trial indicates that it was not fear of disruption that motivated the regulation prohibiting the armbands; the regulation was directed against "the principle of the demonstration" itself. School authorities simply felt that "the schools are no place for demonstrations," and if the students "didn't like the way our elected officials were handling things, it should be handled with the ballot box and not in the halls of our public schools."

4. The District Court found that the school authorities, in prohibiting black armbands, were influenced by the fact that "[t]he Viet Nam war and the involvement of the United States therein has been the subject of a major controversy for some time. When the armband regulation involved herein was promulgated, debate over the Viet Nam war had become vehement in many localities. A protest march against the war had been recently held in Washington, D.C. A wave of draft-

card-burning incidents protesting the war had swept the country. At that time two highly publicized draft-card-burning cases were pending in this Court. Both individuals supporting the war and those opposing it were quite vocal in expressing their views." 258 F. Supp. at 972–973.

5. After the principals' meeting, the director of secondary education and the principal of the high school informed the student that the principals were opposed to publication of his article. They reported that "we felt that it was a very friendly conversation, although we did not feel that we had convinced the student that our decision was a just one."

6. In *Hammond v. South Carolina State College*, 272 F. Supp. 947 (D.C.D.S.C. 1967), District Judge Hemphill had before him a case involving a meeting on campus of 300 students to express their views on school practices. He pointed out that a school is not like a hospital or a jail enclosure. Cf. *Cox v. Louisiana*, 379 U.S. 536 (1965); *Adderley v. Florida*, 385 U.S. 39 (1966). It is a public place, and its dedication to specific uses does not imply that the constitutional rights of persons entitled to be there are to be gauged as if the premises were purely private property. Cf. *Edwards v. South Carolina*, 372 U.S. 229 (1963); *Brown v. Louisiana*, 383 U.S. 131 (1966).

Appendix C

Goss v. Lopez, 419 U.S. 565 (1975)

MR. JUSTICE WHITE delivered the opinion of the Court.

This appeal by various administrators of the Columbus, Ohio, Public School System (CPSS) challenges the judgment of a three-judge federal court, declaring that appellees—various high school students in the CPSS—were denied due process of law contrary to the command of the Fourteenth Amendment in that they were temporarily suspended from their high schools without a hearing either prior to suspension or within a reasonable time thereafter, and enjoining the administrators to remove all references to such suspensions from the students' records.

I

Ohio law, Rev. Code Ann. §3313.64 (1972), provides for free education to all children between the ages of six and 21. Section 3316.66 of the Code empowers the principal of an Ohio public school to suspend a pupil for misconduct for up to 10 days or to expel him. In either case, he must notify the student's parents within 24 hours and state the reasons for his action. A pupil who is expelled, or his parents, may appeal the decision to the Board of Education and in connection therewith shall be permitted to be heard at the board meeting. The board may reinstate the pupil following the hearing. No similar procedure is provided in §3313.66 or any other provision of state law for a suspended student. Aside from a regulation tracking the statute, at the time of the imposition of the suspensions in this case the CPSS itself had not issued any written procedure applicable to suspensions. Nor, so far as the record reflects, had any of the individual high schools involved in this case. Each, however, had formally or informally described the conduct for which suspension could be imposed.

The nine named appellees, each of whom alleged that he or she had been suspended from public high school in Columbus for up to 10 days without a hearing pursuant to §3313.66, filed an action against the Columbus Board of Education and various administrators of the CPSS under 42 U.S.C. §1983. The complaint sought a declaration that §3313.66 was unconstitutional in that it permitted public school administrators to deprive plaintiffs of their rights to an education without a hearing of any kind, in violation of the procedural due process component of the Fourteenth Amendment. It also sought to enjoin the public school officials from issuing future suspensions pursuant to §3313.66 and to require them to remove references to the past suspensions from the records of the students in question.

The proof below established that the suspensions arose out of a period of widespread student unrest in the CPSS during February and March 1971. Six of the named plaintiffs, Rudolph Sutton, Tyrone Washington, Susan Cooper, Deborah Fox, Clarence Byars, and Bruce Harris, were students at the Marion-Franklin High School and were each suspended for 10 days on account of disruptive or disobedient conduct committed in the presence of the school administrator who ordered the suspension. One of these, Tyrone Washington, was among a group of students demonstrating in the school auditorium while a class was being conducted there. He was ordered by the school principal to leave, refused to do so, and was suspended. Rudolph Sutton, in the presence of the principal, physically attacked a police officer who was attempting to remove Tyrone Washington from the auditorium. He was immediately suspended. The other four Marion-Franklin students were suspended for similar conduct. None was given a hearing to determine the operative facts underlying the suspension, but each, together with his or her parents, was offered the opportunity to attend a conference, subsequent to the effective date of the suspension, to discuss the student's future.

Two named plaintiffs, Dwight Lopez and Betty Crome, were students at the Central High School and McGuffey Junior High School, respectively. The former was suspended in connection with a disturbance in the lunchroom which involved some physical damage to school property. Lopez testified that at least 75 other students were suspended from his school on the same day. He also testified below that he was not a party to the destructive conduct but was instead an innocent bystander. Because no one from the school testified with regard to this incident, there is no evidence in the record indicating the official basis for concluding otherwise. Lopez never had a hearing.

Betty Crome was present at a demonstration at a high school other than the one she was attending. There she was arrested together with others, taken to the police station, and released without being formally charged. Before she went to school on the following day, she was notified that she had been suspended for a 10-day period. Because no one from the school testified with respect to this incident, the record does not disclose how the McGuffey Junior High School principal went about making the decision to suspend Crome, nor does it disclose on what information the decision was based. It is clear from the record that no hearing was ever held.

There was no testimony with respect to the suspension of the ninth named plaintiff, Carl Smith. The school files were also silent as to his suspension, although as to some, but not all, of the other named plaintiffs the files contained either direct references to their suspensions or copies of letters sent to their parents advising them of the suspension.

On the basis of this evidence, the three-judge court declared that plaintiffs were denied due process of law because they were "suspended without hearing prior to suspension or within a reasonable time thereafter," and that Ohio Rev. Code Ann. §3313.66 (1972) and regulations issued pursuant thereto were unconstitutional in permitting such suspensions. It was ordered that all references to plaintiffs' suspensions be removed from school files.

Although not imposing upon the Ohio school administrators any particular disciplinary procedures and leaving them "free to adopt regulations providing for fair suspension procedures which are consonant with the educational goals of their schools and reflective of the characteristics of their school and locality," the District Court declared that there were "minimum requirements of notice and a hearing prior to suspension, except in emergency situations." In explication, the court stated that relevant case authority would: (1) permit "[i]mmediate removal of a student whose conduct disrupts the academic atmosphere of the school, endangers fellow students, teachers or school officials, or damages property"; (2) require notice of suspension proceedings to be sent to the student's parents within 24 hours of the decision to conduct them; and (3) require a hearing to be held, with the student present, within 72 hours of his removal. Finally, the court stated that, with respect to the nature of the hearing, the relevant cases required that statements in support of the charge be produced, that the student and others be permitted to make statements in defense or mitigation, and that the school need not permit attendance by counsel.

The defendant school administrators have appealed the three-judge court's decision. Because the order below granted plaintiffs' request for an injunction—ordering defendants to expunge their records—this Court has jurisdiction of the appeal pursuant to 28 U.S.C. §1253. We affirm.

II

At the outset, appellants contend that because there is no constitutional right to an education at public expense, the Due Process Clause does not protect against expulsions from the public school system. This position misconceives the nature of the decision and is refuted by prior decisions. The Fourteenth Amendment forbids the State to deprive any person of life, liberty, or property without due process of law. Protected interests in property are normally "not created by the Constitution. Rather, they are created and their dimensions are defined" by an independent source such as state statutes or rules entitling the citizen to certain benefits.

Accordingly, a state employee who under state law, or rules promulgated by state officials, has a legitimate claim of entitlement to continued employment absent sufficient cause for discharge may demand the procedural protections of due process. . . . So may welfare recipients who have statutory rights to welfare as long as they maintain the specified qualifications. *Morrissey v. Brewer*, 408 U.S. 471 (1972), applied the limitations of the Due Process Clause to governmental decisions to revoke parole, although a parolee has no constitutional right to that status. In like vein was *Wolfe v. McDonnell*, 418 U.S. 539 (1974), where the procedural protections of the Due Process Clause were triggered by official cancellation of a prisoner's good-time credits accumulated under state law, although those benefits were not mandated by the Constitution.

Here, on the basis of state law, appellees plainly had legitimate claims of entitlement to a public education. Ohio Rev. Code Ann. §§3313.48 and 3313.64 (1972 and Supp. 1973) direct authorities to provide a free education to all residents between five and 21 years of age, and a compulsory-attendance law requires attendance for a school year of not less than 32 weeks. Ohio Rev. Code Ann. §3321.04 (1972). It is true that §3313.66 of the code permits school principals to suspend students for up to two weeks; but suspensions may not be imposed without any grounds whatsoever. All of the schools had their own rules specifying the grounds for expulsion or suspension. Having chosen to extend the right to an education to people of appellees' class generally, Ohio may not withdraw that right on grounds of misconduct, absent fundamentally fair procedures to determine whether the misconduct has occurred.

Although Ohio may not be constitutionally obligated to establish and maintain a public school system, it has nevertheless done so and has required its children to attend. Those young people do not "shed their constitutional rights" at the schoolhouse door. *Tinker v. Des Moines School Dist.*, 393 U.S. 503, 506 (1969). "The Fourteenth Amendment, as now applied to the States, protects the citizen against the State itself and all of its creatures—Boards of Education not excepted." *West Virginia Board of Education v. Barnette*, 319 U.S. 624, 637 (1943). The authority possessed by the State to prescribe and enforce standards of conduct in its schools, although concededly very broad, must be exercised consistently with constitutional safeguards. Among other things, the State is constrained to recognize a student's legitimate entitlement to a public education as a property interest which is protected by the Due Process Clause and which may not be taken away for misconduct without adherence to the minimum procedures required by that Clause.

The Due Process Clause also forbids arbitrary deprivations of liberty. "Where a person's good name, reputation, honor, or integrity is at stake because of what the government is doing to him," the minimal requirements of the Clause must be satisfied. School authorities here suspended appellees from school for periods of up to 10 days based on charges of misconduct. If sustained and recorded, those charges could seriously damage the students' standing with their fellow pupils and their teachers as well as interfere with later opportunities for higher education and employment. It is apparent that the claimed right of the State to determine unilaterally and without process whether that misconduct has occurred immediately collides with the requirements of the Constitution.

Appellants proceed to argue that even if there is a right to a public education protected by the Due Process Clause generally, the Clause comes into play only when the State subjects a student to a "severe detriment or grievous loss." The loss of 10 days, it is said, is neither severe nor grievous and the Due Process Clause is therefore of no relevance. Appellants' argument is again refuted by our prior decisions; for in determining "whether due process requirements apply in the first place, we must look not to the 'weight' but to the *nature* of the interest at stake." Appellees were excluded from school only temporarily, it is true, but the length and consequent severity of a deprivation, while another factor to weigh in determining the appropriate form of hearing, "is not decisive of the basic right" to a hearing of some kind. The Court's view has been that as long as a property deprivation is not *de minimis*, its gravity is irrelevant to the question whether account must be taken of the Due Process Clause. A 10-day suspension from school is not *de minimis* in our view and may not be imposed in complete disregard of the Due Process Clause.

A short suspension is, of course, a far milder deprivation than expulsion. But, "education is perhaps the most important function of state and local governments," and the total exclusion from the educational process for more than a trivial period, and certainly if the suspension is for 10 days, is a serious event in the life of the suspended child. Neither the property interest in educational benefits temporarily denied nor the liberty interest in reputation, which is also implicated, is so insubstantial that suspensions may constitutionally be imposed by any procedure the school chooses, no matter how arbitrary.

III

"Once it is determined that due process applies, the question remains what process is due." We turn to that question, fully realizing as our cases regularly do that the interpretation and application of the Due Process Clause are intensely practical matters and that "[t]he very nature of due process negates any concept of inflexible procedures universally applicable to every imaginable situation." We are also mindful of our own admonition that

Judicial interposition in the operation of the public school system of the Nation raises problems requiring care and restraint. . . . By and large, public education in our Nation is committed to the control of state and local authorities.

There are certain bench marks to guide us, however.

A case often invoked by later opinions, said that "[m]any controversies have raged about the cryptic and abstract words of the Due Process Clause but there can be no doubt that at a minimum they require that deprivation of life, liberty or property by adjudication be preceded by notice and opportunity for hearing appropriate to the nature of the case." "The fundamental requisite of due process of law is the opportunity to be heard," a right that "has little reality or worth unless one is informed that the matter is pending and can choose for himself whether to . . . contest." At the very minimum, therefore, students facing suspension and the consequent interference with a protected property interest must be given *some* kind of notice and afforded *some* kind of hearing. "Parties whose rights are to be affected are entitled to be heard; and in order that they may enjoy that right they must first be notified."

It also appears from our cases that the timing and content of the notice and the nature of the hearing will depend on appropriate accommodation of the competing interests involved. The student's interest is to avoid unfair or mistaken exclusion from the educational process, with all of its unfortunate consequences. The Due Process Clause will not shield him from suspensions properly imposed, but it disserves both his interest and the interest of the State if his suspension is in fact unwarranted. The concern would be mostly academic if the disciplinary process were a totally accurate, unerring process, never mistaken and never unfair. Unfortunately, that is not the case, and no one suggests that it is. Disciplinarians, although proceeding in utmost good faith, frequently act on the reports and advice of others; and the controlling facts and the nature of the conduct under challenge are often disputed. The risk of error is not at all trivial, and it should be guarded against if that may be done without prohibitive cost or interference with the educational process.

The difficulty is that our schools are vast and complex. Some modicum of discipline and order is essential if the educational function is to be performed. Events calling for discipline are frequent occurrences and sometimes require immediate, effective action. Suspension is considered not only to be a necessary tool to maintain order but a valuable educational device. The prospect of imposing elaborate hearing requirements in every suspension case is viewed with great concern, and many school authorities may well prefer the untrammeled power to act unilaterally, unhampered by rules about notice and hearing. But it would be a strange disciplinary system in an educational institution if no communication was sought by the disciplinarian with the student in an effort to inform him of his dereliction and to let him tell his side of the story in order to make sure that an injustice is not done. "[F]airness can rarely be obtained by secret, onesided determination of facts decisive of rights. . . ." "Secrecy is not congenial to truth-seeking and self-righteousness gives too slender an assurance of rightness. No better instrument has been devised for arriving at truth than to give a person in jeopardy of serious loss notice of the case against him and opportunity to meet it."

We do not believe that school authorities must be totally free from notice and hearing requirements if their schools are to operate with acceptable efficiency. Students facing temporary suspension have interests qualifying for protection of the Due Process Clause, and due process requires, in connection with a suspension of 10 days or less, that the student be given oral or written notice of the charges against him and, if he denies them, an explanation of the evidence the authorities have and an opportunity to present his side of the story. The Clause requires at least these rudimentary precautions against unfair or mistaken findings of misconduct and arbitrary exclusion from school. There need be no delay between the time "notice" is given and the time of the hearing. In the great majority of cases the disciplinarian may informally discuss the alleged misconduct with the student minutes after it has occurred. We hold only that, in being given an opportunity to

explain his version of the facts at this discussion, the student
first be told what he is accused of doing and what the basis of
the accusation is. Lower courts which have addressed the question of the *nature* of the procedures required in short suspension cases have reached the same conclusion. Since the hearing
may occur almost immediately following the misconduct, it
follows that as a general rule notice and hearing should precede
removal of the student from school. We agree with the District
Court, however, that there are recurring situations in which
prior notice and hearing cannot be insisted upon. Students
whose presence poses a continuing danger to persons or property or an ongoing threat of disrupting the academic process
may be immediately removed from school. In such cases the
necessary notice and rudimentary hearing should follow as soon
as practicable, as the District Court indicated.

In holding as we do, we do not believe that we have imposed
procedures on school disciplinarians which are inappropriate
in a classroom setting. Instead we have imposed requirements
which are, if anything, less than a fair-minded school principal
would impose upon himself in order to avoid unfair suspensions. Indeed, according to the testimony of the principal of
Marion-Franklin High School, that school had an informal procedure, remarkably similar to that which we now require, applicable to suspensions generally but which was not followed
in this case. Similarly, according to the most recent memorandum applicable to the entire CPSS, school principals in the
CPSS are now required by local rule to provide at least as much
as the constitutional minimum which we have described.

We stop short of construing the Due Process Clause to require, countrywide, that hearings in connection with short
suspensions must afford the student the opportunity to secure
counsel, to confront and cross-examine witnesses supporting
the charge, or to call his own witnesses to verify his version
of the incident. Brief disciplinary suspensions are almost countless. To impose in each such case even truncated trial-type
procedures might well overwhelm administrative facilities in
many places and, by diverting resources, cost more than it
would save in educational effectiveness. Moreover, further for-
malizing the suspension process and escalating its formality and
adversary nature may not only make it too costly as a regular

disciplinary tool but also destroy its effectiveness as part of the teaching process.

On the other hand, requiring effective notice and informal hearing permitting the student to give his version of the events will provide a meaningful hedge against erroneous action. At least the disciplinarian will be alerted to the existence of disputes about facts and arguments about cause and effect. He may then determine himself to summon the accuser, permit cross-examination, and allow the student to present his own witnesses. In more difficult cases, he may permit counsel. In any event, his discretion will be more informed and we think the risk of error substantially reduced.

Requiring that there be at least an informal give-and-take between student and disciplinarian, preferably prior to the suspension, will add little to the factfinding function where the disciplinarian himself has witnessed the conduct forming the basis for the charge. But things are not always as they seem to be, and the student will at least have the opportunity to characterize his conduct and put it in what he deems the proper context.

We should also make it clear that we have addressed ourselves solely to the short suspension, not exceeding 10 days. Longer suspensions or expulsions for the remainder of the school term, or permanently, may require more formal procedures. Nor do we put aside the possibility that in unusual situations, although involving only a short suspension, something more than the rudimentary procedures will be required.

IV

The District Court found each of the suspensions involved here to have occurred without a hearing, either before or after the suspension, and that each suspension was therefore invalid and the statute unconstitutional insofar as it permits such suspensions without notice or hearing. Accordingly, the judgment is *Affirmed*.

Selected Bibliography and Information Sources

GENERAL

Access: The Information Clearinghouse about Public Schools. National Committee for Citizens in Education, 10840 Little Pateuxent Parkway, Suite 301, Columbia, MD 21044. Provides fact sheets on rights of students and parents and lists of organizations in each state.

Barriers to Excellence: Our Children at Risk. 1985. National Coalition of Advocates for Students (NCAS), 100 Boylston St., Suite 737, Boston, MA 02116. Final report of the NCAS Board of Inquiry. Focuses on how to achieve excellence in education without sacrificing equity.

CDF Reports. Children's Defense Fund, 122 C St., Washington, DC 20001. Monthly newsletter. Reports on national developments on a wide range of issues affecting young people, including education.

Choosing Equality: The Case for Democratic Schooling. A. Bastian, N. Fruchter, C. Greer, M. Gittell, K. Haskins. 1985. New World Foundation.

Education Law Bulletin. Center for Law and Education, Larsen Hall, 14 Appian Way, Cambridge, MA 02138. Quarterly.

Newsnotes. Center for Law and Education, Larsen Hall, 14 Appian Way, Cambridge, MA 02138.

Steps. National Coalition of Advocates for Students, 100 Boylston St., Suite 737, Boston, MA 02116. Each issue focuses on a different students' rights topic.

Youth Law News. National Center for Youth Law, 1663 Mission St., 5th Floor, San Francisco, CA 94103.

SPECIFIC AREAS

Bilingual Education

"Bilingual Education Programs: A Fundamental Right." Washington Information Resource Center. 1983. Washington, DC: National Congress for Puerto Rican Rights.

Bilingual Education Programs. Printout NC803CP. National Committee for Citizens in Education, 10840 Little Patuexent Parkway, Suite 301, Columbia, MD 21044. Summary of current law, programs, and controversial issues.

Interracial Books for Children Bulletin. Vol. 17, nos. 3–4. 1986. Council on Interracial Books for Children, 1841 Broadway, New York, NY 10023. Special double issue on bilingual education and equity.

Corporal Punishment

Discipline. National Center for the Study of Corporal Punishment and Alternatives in the Schools, 833 Ritter Hall South, Temple University, Philadelphia, PA 19122. Periodical.

Inequality in Education. No. 23, Sept. 1978. Center for Law and Education, Larsen Hall, 14 Appian Way, Cambridge, MA 02138. Special issue on corporal punishment.

"Report of the Task Force on Corporal Punishment." National Education Association, 1201 16th St. N.W., Washington, DC 20036.

Due Process and Discipline

Everybody's Business: A Book about School Discipline. Edited by Joan McCarty First and M. Hayes Mizell. 1980. Southeastern Public Education Program.

School Discipline and Student Rights: An Advocate's Manual. Paul Weckstein. 1982. Center for Law and Education, Larsen Hall, 14 Appian Way, Cambridge, MA 02138.

School Suspensions: Are They Helping Children? Children's Defense Fund, 122 C St. N.W., Washington, DC 20001.

Towards Better and Safer Schools. 1984. National School Boards Association, 1680 Duke St., Alexandria, VA 22314.

First Amendment Rights

Captive Voices: The Report of the Commission into High School Journalism. 1974. New York: Schocken Books.

Student Press Law Center, 800 18th St. N.W., Suite 300, Washington, DC 20006.

School Records

Code of Student Rights and Responsibilities. National Education Association, Academic Building, West Haven, CT 06516.

The Family Educational Rights and Privacy Act Office, Dept. of Education, 330 Independence Ave. S.W., Washington, DC 20201.

Guidelines for the Collection, Maintenance and Dissemination of Pupil Records: Report of a Conference of the Ethical and Legal Aspects of School Board Record Keeping. 1970. Russell Sage Foundation, 230 Park Ave., New York, NY.

Inequality in Education. No. 22, July 1977. Center for Law and Education, Larsen Hall, 14 Appian Way, Cambridge, MA 02138. Special issue on student records.

School Searches and Law Enforcement

The Reasonable Exercise of Authority. Ackerly. National Association of Secondary School Principals, 1201 16th St. N.W., Washington, DC 20036.

"School Metal Detector Searches and the Fourth Amendment: An Empirical Study," Myrna G. Baskin and Laura M. Thomas. *University of Michigan Journal of Law Reform.* Vol. 19, No. 4, Summer 1986.

"Searches of Students by School Officials in Public Schools." William G. Buss. *Inequality in Education.* No. 20, July 1975. Center for Law and Education, Larsen Hall, 14 Appian Way, Cambridge, MA 02138.

Sex Discrimination

The Rights of Women. American Civil Liberties Union Handbook. Susan Deller Ross and Ann Barcher. Revised ed., 1983. Carbondale: Southern Illinois University Press.

Students with Handicapping Conditions

The Rights of Physically Handicapped People. American Civil Liberties Union Handbook. Kent Hull. 1979. New York: Avon Books.

News Digest. National Information Center for Handicapped Children and Youth, Box 1492, Washington, DC 20013. Each issue is devoted to a different topic.

94–142 and 504: Numbers That Add Up to Educational Rights for Handicapped Children: A Guide for Parents and Advocates. 1984. Children's Defense Fund, 122 C St. N.W., Washington, DC 20001.

Special Education: A Manual for Advocates. Diana Pullin. 1982. Center for Law and Education, Larsen Hall, 14 Appian Way, Cambridge, MA 02138.

Special Education: An Overview of Federal Law and Recent Legal Developments. Diana Pullin. 1985. Center for Law and Education, Larsen Hall, 14 Appian Way, Cambridge, MA 02138.

Tracking, Competency Testing, and Hold-overs

"Certifying Functional Literacy." M. Lewis. *Journal of Law and Education.* Vol. 8, April 1979: p. 145.

A Citizen's Introduction to Minimum Competency Programs for Students. 1979. Southeastern Public Education Program, American Friends Service Committee, 401 Columbia Building, Columbia, SC 29201.

Keeping Track: How Schools Structure Inequality. Jeannie Oakes. 1985. New Haven, CT: Yale University Press.

Minimum Competency Testing: A Manual for Legal Services Programs. 1979. Center for Law and Education, Larsen Hall, 14 Appian Way, Cambridge, MA 02138.

"Misuse of Standardized Testing: A Barrier to Excellence." *Steps.* Vol. 1, no. 4, March 1986. National Coalition of Advocates for Students, 100 Boylston St., Suite 737, Boston, MA 02116.

New Promotion and Retention Policies: What They Mean for Children in Your Schools. Page McCullough. Atlantic Center for Research in Education, 604 W. Chapel Hill St., Durham, NC 27701.